PENGUIN BOOKS

THE PEACEFUL ARMY

Penguin Australian Women's Library

Flora Eldershaw was born in Sydney in 1897. She attended Sydney University where she met Marjorie Barnard, who became her literary partner. For twenty years she was a teacher (until the war) and despite the difficulties produced most of her literary work during this period. Flora Eldershaw and Marjorie Barnard, under the pen name of M. Barnard Eldershaw, published the award-winning historical novel, *A House is Built* in 1929. Four more novels followed including the censored *Tomorrow and Tomorrow* (1947) which was not available in its unabridged form until it was republished in 1983 as *Tomorrow and Tomorrow and Tomorrow*. They also published four works of non-fiction, as well as stories and radio plays. In 1935 and again in 1943 she was president of the Sydney branch of the Fellowship of Australian Writers. Her address to the English Teachers' Association—'Australian Women Writers'—was published in 1931 and reveals her support for the validity of Australian literature and for the value of women's contribution within it.

Series Editor: Dale Spender

The Penguin Australian Women's Library will make available to readers a wealth of information through the work of women writers of our past. It will include the classic to the freshly re-discovered, individual reprints to new anthologies, as well as up-to-date critical re-appraisals of their work and lives as writers.

Other books in the Penguin Australian Women's Library

*The Penguin Anthology of Australian Women's Writing*
Edited by Dale Spender

*Mr Hogarth's Will* by Catherine Helen Spence
Introduced by Helen Thomson

*Kirkham's Find* by Mary Gaunt
Introduced by Kylie Tennant
Afterword by Dale Spender

*A Bright and Fiery Troop:*
*Australian Women Writers of the Nineteenth Century*
Edited by Debra Adelaide

*Her Selection:*
*Writings by Nineteenth-Century Australian Women*
Edited by Lynne Spender

Series Editor: Dale Spender
Advisory Board:
Debra Adelaide                Sue Martin
Diane Bell                    Lynne Spender
Sneja Gunew                   Helen Thomson
Elizabeth Lawson

Cover Advisor: Janine Burke

# THE PEACEFUL ARMY

Edited by Dale Spender

PENGUIN BOOKS
Penguin Australian Women's Library

Penguin Books Australia Ltd
487 Maroondah Highway, PO Box 257
Ringwood, Victoria, 3134, Australia
Penguin Books Ltd
Harmondsworth, Middlesex, England
Viking Penguin Inc.
40 West 23rd Street, New York, NY 10010, USA
Penguin Books Canada Limited
2801 John Street, Markham, Ontario, Canada, L3R 1B4
Penguin Books (N.Z.) Ltd
182-190 Wairau Road, Auckland 10, New Zealand

First published by Penguin Books Australia, 1988
Copyright © Foreword is this edition and Afterword Dale Spender
Copyright © this edition Penguin Books Australia, 1988
Copyright © of individual pieces remains with the writers

Typeset in Paladium by Midland Typesetters, Victoria
Made and printed in Australia by Australian Print Group, Victoria

The peaceful army.

ISBN 0 14 011231 6.

1. Women — Australia — Biography. 2. Women pioneers —
Australia — Biography. 3. Women authors — Biography.
4. Women artists — Australia — Biography. I. Eldershaw,
Flora S. (Flora Sydney), 1897-    . (Series: Penguin
Australian women's library).

994'.009'92

# CONTENTS

# FOREWORD TO THE PENGUIN EDITION

As preparations were made to commemorate one hundred and fifty years of white settlement in Australia (the Sesquicentenary of 1938), it became apparent to the Women's Executive Committee and Advisory Council that little credit was being given to the contribution that women had made to the development of the country and the culture. There was a need to recognize publicly the crucial role that they had played in the birth of the nation; one solution proposed was to publish a documentation of women's influence and achievements.

And so the idea for *The Peaceful Army* took shape and the skill and energy of Flora Eldershaw helped to transform the vision into a reality. Elected as president of the Sydney Branch of the Fellowship of Australian Writers in 1935, she used her position, contacts, and talents as a writer, editor and manager, to bring together some of the most outstanding literary and artistic women of the day and to involve them in a project to proclaim the importance of their predecessors.

Writers are well matched with their subjects. The young author Dymphna Cusack, who later earnt for herself a reputation as champion of the oppressed, contributed the chapter on the colourful convict Mary Reiby. The more established novelist Eleanor Dark, well known for her perceptive accounts of individual responsibility, wrote about the pioneering social worker Caroline Chisholm, giving some imaginative glimpses of the woman, her work, and the society she tried to serve.

Miles Franklin who herself had been inspired – and comforted – by Rose Scott, was delighted to present a portrait of this admirable woman. One of the first Australian feminists, one of the most tireless and talented campaigners for votes for women, Rose Scott becomes a heroine with the aid of Miles Franklin's skilful pen.

In outlining the achievements of the gifted women writers of the nineteenth century (Catherine Helen Spence, Ada Cambridge, Rosa Praed, Jessie Couvreur ['Tasma'] and Louisa Atkinson), Winifred Birkett helped to construct Australian women's literary heritage. And Margaret Preston – herself a talented and an acclaimed artist – set the record straight in her own area: she was aware of the valuable contributions of women who had gone before her and was determined to acknowledge her personal debts and to point to the emerging and energizing tradition of women artists in Australia.

In their tributes to these women who forged the impressive literary and artistic heritage, Winifred Birkett and Margaret Preston describe some of the unique Australian conditions in which these women lived and worked, and from which developed an independent and vital cultural milieu.

'M. Barnard Eldershaw' was the pseudonym used by Marjorie Barnard and Flora Eldershaw. 'Pioneers' in their own right, they had become firm friends while attending Sydney University, and their later literary partnership was extraordinarily successful. Their first – and award-winning – novel, *A House is Built* (1929), chronicled the establishment of a family and business in the early years of settlement. Later, when they chose to write about Elizabeth Macarthur – and her family and business – they were able to make links between fact and fiction.

Sadly, their celebration of Elizabeth Macarthur has not made its way into official records for she is still systematically eclipsed by the supposed achievements of her husband.

Marjorie Barnard and Flora Eldershaw, however, would not have been the only contributors who would have been disappointed by this failure to make visible the accomplishments of pioneering women. All of the talented authors in *The Peaceful Army* would have been distressed to learn that their attempts to reclaim their foremothers permanently, and to rightfully reinstate them in the history books, had been less than successful.

Fifty years ago there was a celebration: the initiative of Mary Reiby was applauded, the commitment of Caroline Chisholm commended, Rose Scott was congratulated on her victory, and Elizabeth Macarthur praised for her perseverance. But since that time these exemplary women have once more slipped back into semi-oblivion.

The central theme in Kylie Tennant's chapter is that women's pioneering should and would go on. Fifty years later, just before her own death, she gave this edition her blessing. 'Tell them again and again,' she said, 'just what a wonderful contribution women have made to this society. And tell them why it is crucial that it be remembered.' Kylie Tennant believed that a society that devalued women had little to be proud of, and had but a dubious future.

Some of the women poets of her time shared her views. It was a distinguished band who entered their names and their testimonies, in the pages of *The Peaceful Army*. Some of them are familiar still: Mary Gilmore, Dora Wilcox, Dorothea Mackellar and Helen Simpson, though Olive Hopegood and Kathleen Monypenny are among those who have slipped from notice (neither is included in Debra Adelaide's comprehensive compendium, *Australian Women Writers: A Bibliographic Guide*, 1988, Pandora).

And in 1988 we have two groups of women to reinstate: the early pioneers and the authors of *The Peaceful Army*. For, to this day, neither group enjoys the prestige and prominence it deserves. Not the original women of achievement, not the women who wrote them up. Dymphna Cusack, Eleanor Dark, Miles Franklin, Winifred Birkett, Margaret Preston, Marjorie Barnard, Flora Eldershaw and Kylie Tennant all warrant more attention, greater appreciation.

For the very same reasons that *The Peaceful Army* was published in 1938, it is being reissued in 1988. As the Bicentennial Celebrations proceed, the possibility that women's contribution might once more be eclipsed could be realized. In the words of Kylie Tennant, we must remind ourselves that Australia is indebted not just to 'pioneers and their *wives*' but to the equal and valuable contribution of *pioneering women*. This is a lesson we must learn now and pass on to future generations.

The *Peaceful Army* plays an important role in presenting and preserving this proud record of achievements of Australian women. In fifty years the essays and poems – and the characters – in this volume have not lost their freshness, their fascination, or their relevance.

Dale Spender

# FOREWORD

This book is a tribute from the women of today to the women of yesterday.

Since Australia is happily rich in women pioneers and, as the ever-extending field of women's work and influence is so large, no attempt has been made in this book to record the names and work of all pioneers. Instead, one figure has been chosen to represent each sphere of women's endeavour; her story has been told and the background drawn in some detail. Many others could, with equal justice, have been chosen, but we hope that through these few some picture of the whole will emerge. These are the standard-bearers, though not necessarily the leaders, of the peaceful army.

In two fields only, in art and in literature, have we included group surveys, and in these only have we gone beyond the confines of New South Wales.

For the literary sub-committee,
Flora S. Eldershaw, editor

*Literary sub-committee*:
Dame Mary Gilmore          Marjorie Barnard
Dora Wilcox                Flora Eldershaw
Miles Franklin

# MARY GILMORE

## Ode to the Pioneer Women

O braiding thought, move out – move on!
Twine, Memory, your golden thread!
Marble, be monument to them –
Our homage here their diadem –
Lest, as with nations long since gone,
We lose the names should be our bread.

Call them, Australia! Call them once again,
For they are those who on these shores first stood;
Women upon whose long endurings rest
The might and majesty acclaimed by us today.

They are the women who by lonely doorsteps sat,
And heard with inward ears the throstle and
The nightingale that they would never hear again,
Who saw as in a dream
The little corncrake in dim distant fields,
Or talked of moons of silver as they watched
The torrid rising of our orb of gold.
And though with wistful longing they looked back,
And knew (so oft!) the sudden tear of memory,
They bore the burden of the strange – they who had never known
But homely things: the dovecot by the barn;
The skep beside the door; the kindly thatch
That covered them; the woodbine and the rose;
The singing of the lark, that, all day long,
Thrilled out above the gorse his jewelled song.

O firmaments of time,
Where planets ages are,

Ye shall the past sublime
  And set each name a star.

For these were they who came –
  A cockle shell for ship –
Daring the sun's red flame,
  And the wind's wild whip.

The vast about them lay,
  The unknown walled them round,
Like doors, that knew no way,
  Loneliness was their bound.

Theirs but a grain of wheat,
  Theirs but the small frail hand,
But they gave the race to eat,
  And they made the land.

The handless dreamer wasteful sits among his dreams
While worlds about him fall. These, too, had dreams.
But theirs were dreams of homes, of hope and pride:
And these they braced with deeds!
  They were the sainted ones – haloed by courage,
As by endurance they were crowned.
For they were women who at need took up
And plied the axe, or bent above the clodded spade;
Who herded sheep; who rode the hills, and brought
The half-wild cattle home – helpmates of men,
Whose children lay within their arms,
Or at the rider's saddle-pommel hung,
And at whose knees, by night, were said familiar prayers.
Ah! Though the towers of Ilium topped the skies,
Yet here were women rising higher still.
Of such as these was born the Anzac and his pride.

If ever in the dark embrace
Of fear it is our lot to stand,
Vouchsafe, O God, to us this grace:
That we may be as those who stood,
Lone on the threshold of this land,
In their enduring womanhood.

# M. BARNARD ELDERSHAW

## The Happy Pioneer – Elizabeth Macarthur

### I
### *The Voyage*

The exact date of Elizabeth Veale's marriage to John Macarthur is not recorded. It lies somewhere between 1784 and 1788. It was not an event that called for much attention beyond the family circle, for it was far from a brilliant match on either side. The bride was the daughter of a small landowner of Holdsworthy, on the the borders of Cornwall and Devonshire; she was very young (in 1789, when they sailed for Australia, she was barely twenty-one), and was considered by her own family to be a 'timid and irresolute girl'. The young bridegroom – he was under thirty – erred in the opposite direction; his temper was proud and his manner often overbearing, although his fortune and position in life did little to support these traits. He came of a fighting and rebellious stock, for he was the second son of Alexander Macarthur, the sole survivor of seven brothers who fought for Bonnie Prince Charlie at Culloden Moor. Alexander escaped from England and lived in the West Indies until it was safe to return home. Eventually he settled in Plymouth as an army agent, married, and there his children were born. When in 1783 John Macarthur went to live at Holdsworthy, he was at a loose end. He had been retired from the army at the end of the wars in 1783 – on ensign's half pay – and was studying agriculture. He also had leanings towards the law, and spent much of his time reading law and history, chiefly English and Roman. The marriage to Elizabeth Veale must have been a love match, and evidently relatives and friends did not scruple to label it foolish and improvident, for later Elizabeth Macarthur wrote to her girlhood friend, Elizabeth Kingdon:

'I offer in myself an instance that it is not always, with all our wise foreseeings, those marriages which promise most or least happiness, prove in their result such as our friends may predict. Few of mine, I am certain, when I married thought that either of us had taken a prudent step. I was considered indolent and inactive; Mr Macarthur too proud and haughty for our humble fortune or expectations, and yet see how bountifully Providence has dealt with us.'

A partnership that was to prove of national importance had been entered into.

John Macarthur decided to stay in the army, and in 1788 he was appointed to the 68th (Durham) Regiment, and in the following year he volunteered for the New South Wales Corps then forming. His first child, Edward, had been born, and with additional incentive to get on in the world, Macarthur wanted something more stimulating than the slow process of advancement in the army in peacetime. He got his step at once. He was appointed lieutenant on 5 June 1789. He also obtained permission to take his wife and child with him. Only one other officer was to be accompanied by his wife, Abbott, the senior lieutenant of the corps.

Elizabeth was eager for the adventure. She wrote to her mother from Chatham Barracks on 8 October 1789:

'In my last letter I informed you, my dear mother, of my husband's exchange into a corps destined for New South Wales, from which we have every reasonable expectation of reaping the most material advantages. You will be surprised that even I, who appear timid and irresolute, should be a warm advocate for this scheme. So it is, and believe me I shall be greatly disappointed if anything happens to impede it. I foresee how terrific and gloomy this will appear to you. To me at first it had the same appearance, while I suffered myself to be blinded by common and vulgar prejudices. I have not now, nor I trust shall ever have one scruple or regret, but what relates to you.'

This was an act of faith on the young Elizabeth's part, of faith in her husband chiefly. The colony had been founded a little over two years. Apart from Governor Phillip's measured hopefulness, the reports that had come home in the First Fleet were not encouraging. The land offered every obstruction and no sustenance. It was beautiful, but strange and unwelcoming. It might be dangerous; the blacks were uncertain; the majority of the colonists were convicts, for whom not very adequate guards had been provided. Life was very rough, and must remain so for years to come. Lastly, the voyage out was long and perilous, and once arrived there was no retreat. Yet Macarthur does not seem to have hesitated to take his young wife and child with him. He could not as yet have had any plans for the conquest of a new world; Australia was still too much a *terra incognita*, but his vigorous and hopeful temperament, impatient of the restrictions of the old world, hoped everything from the new.

They embarked in the *Neptune*, the most notorious ship in the notorious Second Fleet, on 13 November 1789, but it was 17 January before they actually sailed. There were endless delays and inconveniences. The family had not been in the ship a day when Macarthur quarrelled with the master, Gilbert, which 'precluded all further communication between him and Mr Macarthur'. When the ship put into Plymouth they went ashore and fought a duel, from which neither apparently suffered any damage. Mrs Macarthur left the ship to pay a last visit to her mother, but was brought back in the middle of the night by a report, issued by the master, that the *Neptune* was about to sail. This was too much. Captain Nepean, of the corps, who was sailing in her and had also been hoaxed, complained to the owners, and Gilbert was replaced by Donald Traill. 'Experience soon taught us a very disagreeable truth,' laments Elizabeth; 'Mr Traill's character was of a much blacker dye than was ever in Mr Gilbert's nature to exhibit.'

On 8 January 1790, the *Neptune* sailed, but was turned back by bad weather, and anchored at the Motherbank for another week. The 17th saw her final departure, and she ran straight into a heavy storm in the Bay of Biscay. 'For the first time, I began to be a coward,' Elizabeth wrote in her journal.

She had every cause for fear and unhappiness. The *Neptune* was a transport, crowded with convicts and badly found. Macarthur was soon at loggerheads with the master and, more serious still, with Captain Nepean, who sided with Traill. Captain Nepean, said Elizabeth tartly, adopted 'that very generous maxim, every man for himself'. The Macarthurs' cabin was separated only by a thin partition from the women convicts' quarters, so that they were constantly aware of their unhappy neighbours and in constant dread of the fevers and diseases rife among the women. Their only exit was through a dark and noisome passage, used and slept in by the convicts, which Elizabeth dared not use for fear of infection. 'Thus precluded from the general advantage that even the convicts enjoyed, air and exercise, no language can express, no imagination conceive, the misery I experienced.' Their maid fell ill of a gaol fever, and before the ship was a fortnight on its way little Edward was taken very ill, 'and continued in the most pitiable weak state during our passage to the Cape'. The heat of the tropics made conditions worse.

'Approaching near the equator (where the heat in the best situations is almost insupportable), assailed with noisome stenches that even in the cold of an English winter hourly diffusions of oil of tar in my cabin could not dispel, two sides of it being surrounded with wretches whose dreadful imprecations and shocking discourses ever rang in my distracted ears, a sickly infant constantly claiming maternal cares, my spirits failing, my health forsaking me, nothing but the speedy change which took place could have prevented me from falling helpless victim to the unheard-of inhumanity of a set of monsters whose triumph and pleasure seemed to consist in aggravating my distresses.'

The 'speedy change' was transfer to another ship, the *Scarborough*. A quarrel between Macarthur and Nepean over the soldiers' rations brought matters to a head. Permission to transfer was readily given. They were much more comfortable aboard this ship, where they shared quarters with Lieutenant and Mrs Abbott; but their troubles were not over. At Cape Town Macarthur got soaked in the surf one windy day as he was embarking some drunken soldiers for the transport. He contracted rheumatic fever. 'It continued to rage till every sense was lost and every faculty but life destroyed,' wrote Elizabeth; 'and my little boy at that time was so very ill that I could scarcely expect him to survive a day. Alone, unfriended, and in such a situation, what do I not owe to a merciful God for granting me support and assistance in these severe moments of affliction.'

The rest of the voyage appears to have been uneventful, and the *Scarborough* made Port Jackson at the end of June 1790, a very speedy voyage for those days. When Elizabeth stepped ashore, she left the most arduous part of her pioneering behind her. This voyage, and its distresses, was crucial in her life; it changed her from a gentle, indeterminate girl into a woman of character. It hardened and strengthened her, and bred in her a will to survive equal to her husband's. It fitted her for the part she was to play, and it is for that reason that I have dwelt on it at such length. Certainly she suffered, but never once in the diary and the letters that remain to us does she express pity for or sympathy with the convicts who shared the terrible journey with her, and whose sufferings were so much greater than her own. There were tragic scenes in Sydney Cove when the convicts were disembarked from the Second Fleet. They were emaciated with starvation and disease; many were too weak to help themselves, and had to be lowered into the boats in slings like cargo; many died before they could be brought ashore. The masters had starved the convicts so that they might sell their rations at famine prices in Sydney. The worst of them, Donald Traill, was brought to trial for it, and the scandal rang through England – but not loudly enough.

## II
## Husband and Wife

Elizabeth Macarthur's first years in Australia appear to have been very happy ones. She has left in her letters a cheerful record of them. It was a brand-new world, and she was full of eager curiosity. The colony had been established only three and a half years when she landed, and everything was in a very primitive state. She saw a magnificent harbour with many winding, thickly wooded inlets, and on one of its coves a small settlement, a collection of makeshift huts for the most part, into which the methodical governor was trying to bring some order and semblance of dignity. Westward of the settlement the bush stretched in an apparently unbroken wall to the range of mountains that showed pale blue on the horizon. Sixteen miles away, on another branch of the harbour, where the soil was better, there was another small settlement, called Rose Hill.

When the Second Fleet made port, Sydney was in the grip of a famine. Everyone from the governor down was on a common weekly ration of 2 lb salt pork, 2½ lb flour, and 2 lb rice. Clothing, too, was almost exhausted. Scarcely a soldier had a pair of boots to his feet, and the convicts were going round like scarecrows in any rags they could find. The Second Fleet, with its burden of sick and dying humanity, did little to relieve conditions, but it did break the grip of depression on the starving community. It had believed itself forgotten and abandoned by England; now communication was established once more, and the ships brought enough food to give a little relief.

It was not then a very hopeful world into which the Macarthurs stepped, but they were as comfortably placed as anyone. Elizabeth had few complaints. She was interested in everything, the climate was perfect – she had never known such bright, warm winter weather – and little Edward, who, although over a year old now, was not as developed as a normal child of four months, began to improve rapidly. Socially Elizabeth had a great success. She was the only lady, it is said, who was invited to the parties at Government House. (What, one wonders, had become of Mrs Abbott, the senior lieutenant's wife, and Mrs Johnson, the chaplain's wife?) Governor Phillip was, in the phrase of the time, very attentive. The vice-regal dinner parties were for the most part a feast of soul, as the governor had turned his private stocks of food into the public store, and only the ordinary ration was served there, albeit dressed by a French chef. Gentlemen were expected to bring their own bread, but 'there is always a roll for Mrs Macarthur'.

Of her daily life at this time Mrs Macarthur wrote to her friend in England, Miss Kingdon:

'We passed our time away for many weeks cheerfully, if not gaily – gaily indeed it could not be said to be. On my first landing everything was new to me, every Bird, every Insect, Flower, etc., in short, all was novelty around me, and was noticed with a degree of eager curiosity and perturbation, that after a while subsided into that calmness I have already described.'

Her chief care was to find some occupation. They became very friendly with the young officers of the garrison which the NSW Corps was to replace, especially with the accomplished and charming Captain Tench and the more studious Lieutenant Dawes.

'Mr Dawes we do not see so frequently. He is so much engaged with the stars that to mortal eye he is not always visible. I had the presumption to become his pupil, and meant to learn a little astronomy. It is true I have many pleasant walks to his house (something less than half a mile from Sydney), have given him much trouble in making orreries, and explaining to me the general principles of the heavenly bodies, but I soon found I had mistaken my abilities and blush at my error. Still I wanted something to fill up a certain vacancy in my time, which could neither be done by writing, reading, or conversation. To the two first I did not feel myself always inclined, and the latter was not in my power, having no female friend to unbend my mind to, nor a single woman with whom I could converse with any satisfaction to myself . . . These considerations made me still anxious to learn some easy science to fill up the vacuum of many a solitary day, and at length, under the auspices of Mr Dawes, I have made a small progress in botany. No country can exhibit a more copious field for botanical knowledge than this. I am arrived so far as to be able to class and order all common plants. I have found great pleasure in my study; every walk furnished me with subjects to put in practice that Theory I had before gained by reading . . .'

Elizabeth had not long to complain of too little to do. The *Gorgon*, man-of-war, arrived with sufficient stores aboard to give the struggling settlement a new lease of life. The arrival also gave a fillip to social life, as, besides the officers of the ship, Captain Parker had brought his wife, and Phillip Gidley King and Mrs King were aboard, en route for Norfolk Island to resume the governorship. There were dinner parties at Government House and excursions on the harbour, and Mrs Macarthur was happy in the company of 'acceptable females' at last. In December the *Gorgon* sailed, taking with her most of the officers of the marine detachment, including Captain Tench and Lieutenant Dawes. The little society was left desolate, but Elizabeth had little time to lament, for her husband was seriously ill throughout December, and in January they moved into a new and more commodious home. Her family was increasing too. Elizabeth, her eldest daughter, was born in Australia, and a boy, James, who died when he was eleven months old. She had her hands full, but the elegancies were not quite forgotten. Mr Worgan, who came out as surgeon in the *Sirius*, Phillip's flagship, left Elizabeth his piano, on which he had taught her to play.

'Our new house is ornamented with a pianoforte of Mr Worgan's; he kindly means to leave it with me, and now, under his direction, I have begun a new study, but I fear without my master I shall not make any great proficiency. I am told, however, that I have done wonders in being able to play off God Save the King and Foot's Minuet, besides that of reading the notes with great facility.'

She took a keen interest, too, in the events of the small world around her: the attempts at exploration westward, always repelled by the wildness of the country and the scarcity of water; the natives, especially the woman Daringa, in whom she discovered 'a softness and gentleness of manner . . . truly interesting', and whom she took under her protection; the plight of Norfolk Island, cut off for so many months from the parent settlement by the wreck of the *Sirius* . . .

How circumscribed her world was is illustrated by a passage from a letter to Miss Kingdon in March 1791:

'Of my walks round Sydney the longest has not extended beyond three miles, and that distance I have, I believe, only ventured upon twice: once to a farm which Captain Nepean has for his Company, to which we sent our tea equipage and drank tea on the turf, and once to a hill situated between this and Botany Bay, where I could command a prospect of that famous spot. Nor do I think there is any probability of my seeing much of the inland country until it is cleared, as beyond a certain distance round the Colony there is nothing but native paths, very narrow and very incommodious.'

The summer of 1790 to 1791 was very hot and dry. The Tank Stream, which was Sydney's water supply, was running low, and there was a good deal of anxiety about it. Hot northerly winds scourged the country, and the birds were dropping dead from the trees. A plague of flying foxes came to Rose Hill, and, perishing from the heat, polluted the water supply. Mrs Macarthur shut herself in her house, bearing it as best she could, cowering in terror before the violent storms that at last broke the drought and cooled the air. But she was happy. She could write: 'I can with truth add for myself, that since I have had the powers of reason and reflection I never was more sincerely happy than at this time.'

This was a placid period socially, too, for Macarthur was on good terms with Phillip and seems to have had no quarrel on hand. Even the old enmity with Nepean was healed over. 'He is truly a good-hearted man,' wrote Elizabeth, 'and has, I believe, a great friendship for Mr Macarthur.' In June 1791, Macarthur was transferred to Rose Hill, now beginning to be called Parramatta, in the course of his duty, and the first note of discontent is heard. Elizabeth wrote to her mother in the November of that year: 'Parramatta may have advantages, particularly to such as wish to cultivate the land, but officers have so little encouragement in this respect that few will in future attempt it, as evident impediments are thrown in the way to check their undertaking it.' It was against Phillip's policy to grant land to officers, as he thought a stake in the country would draw away their attention from their duties. Macarthur began to chafe. His profession did not offer sufficient scope for his energies. He had always been interested in agriculture, too, and here was a great plenitude of land, but none for him.

At the end of 1792 all that was changed. Phillip resigned his governorship on account of ill-health, and the commandant of the New South Wales Corps, first Grose, then Paterson, ruled as lieutenant-governor. The age of privilege had begun. Grose granted Macarthur a hundred acres at Parramatta. He offered a further grant of a hundred acres to the first officer who got fifty under cultivation. Macarthur won the prize. He had begun his career as a landowner, and Elizabeth was made happy by the gift from Grose of a cow and calf. 'To a family in this country in its present situation it is a gift beyond value that can be placed upon it.'

In three years they were settled at Elizabeth Farm and prospering exceedingly. Elizabeth was writing to her mother on 23 August 1794: 'I write to you now from our own house, a very excellent brick building, 68 feet in length and 18 feet in width, independent of kitchen and servants' apartments. I thank God we enjoy all the comfort we could desire.' At the same time Macarthur wrote to his brother in England a full description of his property, and it is interesting to glimpse it, a self-contained little world, something like a medieval manor, set in a wilderness which to Macarthur almost alone bristled with opportunities.

'I have a farm containing nearly 250 acres, of which upwards of 100 are under cultivation, and the greater part of the remainder is cleared of the timber which grows upon it. Of this year's produce I have sold £400 worth, and I have now remaining in my Granaries upwards of 1800 bushels of corn . . . My stock consists of a horse, 2 mares, 2 cows, 130 goats, upwards of 100 hogs. Poultry of all kinds I have in the greatest abundance . . . With the assistance of one man and half a dozen greyhounds, which I keep, my table is constantly supplied with wild duck and kangaroos. Averaging one week with another these dogs do not kill less than 300 lb weight.' As for the house: 'It has no upper storey, but consists of four rooms on the ground floor, a large hall, closets, cellar, etc.; adjoining is a kitchen, with servants' apartments, and other necessary offices. The house is surrounded by a vineyard and garden of about three acres, the former full of vines and fruit trees, and the latter abounding with most excellent vegetables.'

The young couple had entered on a patriarchal form of existence, with everything in their favour. The land they received as a gift, most of their labour was assigned, a market for all their produce and at a high price was assured, for the governor favoured his officers when it came to allotting government contracts. Grain brought ten shillings a bushel and beef four shillings to five shillings a pound, while a horse was worth from a hundred and forty to a hundred and fifty pounds and a cow about eighty pounds. It was not long either before Macarthur and his brother officers embarked on another form of lucrative trade. 'The officers in the colony, with a few others possessed of money or credit in England, unite together and purchase the cargoes of such vessels as repair to this country from various quarters. Two or more are chosen from their numbers to bargain for the cargo offered for sale, which is then divided among them, in proportion to the amount of their subscriptions. This arrangement,' Mrs Macarthur innocently adds, 'prevents monopoly and the impositions which would be otherwise practised by masters of ships.' She goes on: 'This country possesses numerous advantages to persons holding appointments under government.'

These were bad days for the colony, but very good days for the officers of the NSW Corps who governed the country. Macarthur, the most energetic of them, added the appointment of superintendent of agriculture and paymaster of his regiment to his other activities.

With the appointment of Hunter to the governorship in 1795, Macarthur received his first check. Hunter was pledged to curb the power of the corps and to put down the rum traffic, which had grown to alarming proportions under the rule of the commandants. Macarthur soon fell out with the governor on a matter of policy and resigned his superintendentship. It was in the year of this quarrel – a very spirited affair – that Macarthur first began to interest himself in sheep. He had among his livestock some Bengal sheep, goatlike animals with hairy coats. To these, in the fortuitous style of the day, he added some Irish ewes. The cross resulted in a mixture of hair and wool. This interested Macarthur, and in 1796 he imported some merino sheep from the Cape. He kept them apart, and experimented in wool with ever-increasing success. So almost simultaneously were founded the two great interests of Macarthur's life, quarrelling with governors and growing wool, a most dangerous and a most peaceful pursuit. To these interests his wife's life was bound with his.

In 1800 Macarthur got leave to visit England to seek support from the government for his woolgrowing. He took with him his seven-year-old son John and little Elizabeth. Edward had already been sent home – 'my dear Edward almost quitted me without a tear'. It was one of Mrs Macarthur's greatest griefs that she had to part so early from her children, but there was no means of educating them as family ambition decreed in New South Wales. John she was never to see again. He died thirty years later in London, in the midst of a promising career at the Bar.

In 1801 Macarthur returned, bringing little Elizabeth, who was too delicate to endure the English climate, and a governess, Penelope Lucas, who was to be his wife's firm friend for the next thirty years. She taught the three daughters of the house, Elizabeth, Mary and Emmeline, so their mother was able to keep them at home.

As soon as he returned, Macarthur ran into storms. He quarrelled with Governor King, a more masterful man than Hunter, whose object was to curtail the privileges of the corps within reasonable limits. Colonel Paterson, because he refused to boycott the governor, also evoked Macarthur's ire. They fought a duel, and Paterson was wounded in the shoulder. King arrested Macarthur and sent him to England for court-martial. He was rebuked and ordered to return at once to duty without trial. He resigned from the army and sold his commission, now the senior captaincy of the corps. King was also rebuked.

Macarthur did not return until 1805, but he had not been idle. On the whole things had gone well with him in England. He made an enemy of Sir Joseph Banks, it is true, and laid up much future trouble for himself, but Lord Camden listened with interest to his projects. There was a serious wool famine. Spain supplied most of the fine wool but could not produce as much as the English manufacturers needed to fill their orders. Camden instructed King to grant Macarthur five thousand acres of the best land then available, the cowpastures. (The grant was originally ten thousand acres, but Banks had it whittled down to five thousand, the other five thousand to be granted later.) Macarthur bought some merino sheep from the King's flock. There is a record of the sale: 'Lot 6. A very lively sheep was bought by Captain Macarthur at £11,' and so on. Even at the sheep sale he had a brush with Sir Joseph Banks. Macarthur chartered a ship, renamed her the *Argo*, gave her a golden fleece for a figurehead, and put his sheep, some olive plants, grape vines, and a great many other things aboard. Banks made an effort to stop the sailing on a point of law, but Macarthur got a warrant from Lord Camden and triumphantly set off for home, accompanied by his nephew, Hannibal Macarthur, and two wool-sorters.

In the meantime Mrs Macarthur had been managing their flourishing estate. She had her hands full with her household, the management of the dairy, supervision of the livestock, especially the sheep, about which her husband was so particular, and which, perhaps to her disgust, were far too precious ever to become mutton for the family table, and the farming. She looked on the world about her and found it good. A little while before she had written a description of the countryside to Miss Kingdon:

'It is now spring, and the eye is delighted with the most beautiful variegated landscape. Almonds, apricots, pear and apple trees are in full bloom. The native shrubs are also in flower, and the whole countryside gives a grateful perfume. There is a very good carriage road now made from hence (Parramatta) to Sydney, which by land is distant about 14 miles, and another from this to the river Hawkesbury, which is about 20 miles . . . The road is through uninterrupted wood, with the exception of the village of Toongabbie . . . The greater part of the country is like an English park, and the trees give it the appearance of a wilderness or shrubbery, commonly attached to the habitations of people of fortune, filled with a variety of native plants, placed in a wild, irregular manner. I was at the Hawkesbury three days. It is a noble freshwater river, taking its rise in a precipitous range of mountains that it has hitherto been impossible to pass; many attempts have been made, although in vain. I spent an entire day on this river, going in a boat to a beautiful spot named by the late Governor Richmond Hill, high and overlooking a great extent of country. On one side are those stupendous barriers to which I have alluded, rising as it were immediately above your head; below the river itself, still and unruffled; out of sight is heard a waterfall, whose distant murmurs add awfulness to the scene.'

When her husband returned with the largest land grant yet bestowed in his pocket, their life in Australia entered a new and wider stage. It was a bitter pill for King to have to reward his antagonist with five thousand acres, but he appears to have done it with a good grace, and, though he disapproved of the area selected, to have increased the number of assigned servants allotted to Macarthur. The land was eventually allotted in two parcels, one of two thousand, two hundred and fifty acres, the other at two thousand, seven hundred and fifty acres, both in the cowpastures, but divided by Walter Davidson's estate, Belmont, which Macarthur subsequently bought at four pounds an acre. He had also acquired earlier Foveaux's three thousand acres near Toongabbie, so even at this date he held more land than any other private individual in Australia.

Bligh replaced King as Governor in 1806, and Mrs Macarthur notes an immediate decay of the pioneers' fair prospects. 'Food, clothing and every necessary of life bears a price truly astonishing,' she wrote to Miss Kingdon in January 1807. 'All these melancholy changes may be considered the effect of tyranny and an improper administration of law. Liberty has retired from among us into the pathless wilds, among the poor native inhabitants, who certainly maintain their independence, and have hitherto resisted any infringement on their rights.'

Bligh was a protégé of Sir Joseph Banks, and came to the colony with a prejudice against Macarthur which quickly bore fruit. He looked on Macarthur as the root of the trouble with the NSW Corps, which he had been sent out to settle, and acted accordingly. The story is too well known to need re-telling. The crisis came when the corps, under Major Johnston, marched on Government House, arrested Bligh, and declared him deposed from his governorship. That night Macarthur wrote to Elizabeth: 'I have been deeply engaged all this day in contending for the liberties of this unhappy Colony, and I am happy to say I have succeeded beyond what I expected . . . The Tyrant is now no doubt gnashing his teeth with vexation at his overthrow. May he often have cause to do the like.'

Naturally Elizabeth was wholeheartedly on her husband's side in this quarrel. Johnston, and then his senior officer, Foveaux, acted as governor, and Macarthur was secretary of the state without salary. Both parties to the dispute bombarded the home government with explanations and accusations. Government, hearing both sides, was not anxious to have the story made public, but Johnston pressed for a trial. In 1809 he went to England, accompanied by Macarthur. Government supported Bligh, though he was never employed again, and Johnston was cashiered. Macarthur was not tried, but for nearly nine years he was refused permission to return to Australia.

## III
### Elizabeth Macarthur Alone

This time Macarthur took with him his two younger sons, James (called after his dead brother) and William. Mrs Macarthur was left for the next nine years – crucial ones in the Australian sheep industry – to manage a large estate in a world that was no longer Arcadian. Her eldest son, Edward, who by now had finished his education, elected to go into the army; her second son was destined for the law. The responsibility for the family fortunes rested on her, but she proved the better businessman. She had anxieties other than those of business. Her daughter Elizabeth was an invalid, and at the time of Macarthur's sailing was so dangerously ill that she was hardly expected to recover.

Unfortunately Elizabeth Macarthur's letters to her husband at this time, which would be so illuminating, have not survived, but his to her still exist, and have in large part been made available. They show the high value that that masterful man set on her ability.

'I am perfectly aware, my beloved wife, of the difficulties you have to contend with, and fully convinced that not one woman in a thousand (no one that I know) would have resolution and perseverance to contend with them all, much more to surmount them in the manner that you have so happily done. That I am grateful and delighted with your conduct I think it is needless for me to say, because the consciousness you must feel how impossible it is, that such exemplary goodness can have failed to produce that effect, must convince you I am so, more certainly than any assurance that can be given. May God Almighty reward you both in this world and the next, and may the remainder of your life be free from those cruel cares and sorrows that have chequered so many of the last ten years.'

The letters contain many more passages in this vein. He never questions her judgement or regrets any of her arrangements, but sometimes he is distinctly cross because she does not send him fuller statements about the property. 'Many important things escape your memory at the moment of writing – do adopt the practice of making short memos when anything occurs worth repeating – I much wish for regular sale accounts of stock. When I am asked the price of stock, which I frequently am, I know not what to say. Inform me upon what terms you sold Hannibal the flock of sheep and include the Horses in your next returns.'

Mrs Macarthur's days were full of practical matters; her husband had plenty of time to savour his impotence, and not to know how his affairs stood put a still sharper edge on his inability to conduct them. The difficulties of communication were also very great. In January 1813, Macarthur was writing: 'I am still without any letter from you of a later date than November 1811.' As New South Wales was served in those days by ships of the East India Company, calling in on their outward voyage, letters and packets generally arrived in England via India or China, and were exposed to many risks, from forgetfulness to shipwreck. Most letters were committed to friends, for postage was exorbitant, and was paid by the recipient. Letters from home via Rio cost Macarthur nine pounds and ten shillings and some others, posted on from Portsmouth only, cost four pounds and ten shillings. Elizabeth in her exuberance often forgot how expensive these things were, and he was always entreating her, 'Whenever newspapers are sent a special charge should be given to the person to whom they are entrusted not to send them by post, and all superfluous covers on Letters should be avoided.'

Macarthur had good reason to fear that a premature return would ruin him. (To return would have been a difficult matter in any case as he was not allowed aboard any government ship, and few others came to Australia from England.) Macquarie had succeeded to the governorship ('I know a little of Colonel McQuarry and think him a Gentlemanly Man') and he had the following instruction from Castlereagh:

'You are to take immediate measures for putting Major Johnston in close arrest and for sending him home in order that he may be tried and, as Governor Bligh has represented that Mr Macarthur has been the leading Promoter and Instigator of the mutinous measures which have been taken against His Majesty's Government, you will, if examinations be sworn against him charging him with criminal acts against the Governor and his authority, have him arrested thereupon and brought to trial before the Criminal Court of the Colony.' Government was content to leave him alone so long as he remained out of the colony. By no means could he get the instruction rescinded. Mrs Macarthur, who was on friendly terms at Government House, had the delicate mission of trying to persuade Macquarie, through Mrs Macquarie, to ask government to permit her husband's return. Macquarie, with no abatement of friendliness, evaded the issue. In August 1816, Lord Bathurst, then colonial secretary, agreed to Macarthur's return on condition that he admitted his 'impropriety of conduct' in the Bligh affair. This Macarthur would not do so there was another deadlock. But in the following February he received permission to depart. Late at night, alone, by candlelight, and much shaken by joy, he wrote the good news to his wife.

They had been eight unhappy years for Macarthur. His health had been bad, severe chills, heart attacks and 'flying gout', no doubt an inheritance from the rheumatic fever he had contracted on his first voyage, had succeeded one another. He had felt the separation from his wife and daughters bitterly. 'Believe me, my Elizabeth, the period of my separation from you has been an almost uninterrupted scene of indescribable wretchedness. If the Almighty shall be graciously pleased to bestow upon me any future blessings it can only be in your society.' So active a man felt, too, the separation from his interests. He believed that Europe was doomed – this was towards the end of the Napoleonic wars – and England on the verge of a revolution. 'The country is ruined' was his perpetual cry. To him Australia seemed the Promised Land, the one haven of peace and plenty left in the world. All it needed for prosperity was a staple commodity for export, wool. He worked for the wool industry in England. It was his consuming interest.

The years of separation were much happier for Mrs Macarthur. She had work to do. She not only managed the estate but carried out land deals, all with the object of consolidating and extending the estate at Camden, and disposed of the speculative cargoes Macarthur sent out from England. When, worn down by his exile, Macarthur thought of selling his Australian property and removing his family to England, he left the final decision to her, and she decided to remain in the colony. He was to recognise her decision as the right one. Elizabeth Macarthur's sentiments, as well as her interests, were now centred in Australia.

The colony was making strides now, and Mrs Macarthur resented the restrictions which the greater sophistication of life and the complication of government set upon the patriarchal life. She looked with suspicion on all government interference, especially taxes. From her letters to Miss Kingdon and from letters from Hannibal Macarthur to his uncle we get glimpses of her daily life and of public events as they appeared to contemporary landowners. She does not appear to have been victimized on account of her husband's rash politics but was often a guest at Government House. Macquarie she found 'one of the most pleasing men', and Mrs Macquarie 'is very amiable, very benevolent, in short, a very good woman'. There was more social life in Sydney now. 'On particular days, such as the King's or Queen's birthday, there are parties at Government House, numbering occasionally 150 persons. I will not say that these assemblies have been very select, however, there is a sufficiency of pleasant, agreeable persons to visit and be visited by to satisfy one who is not ambitious to have a very numerous visiting acquaintance.'

She watched Macquarie's two hundred buildings rise and notes with pleasure that 'three gentlemen' have crossed the Blue Mountains at last. (It was the sheep industry founded by her husband that made it imperative for the colony to break through that barrier.) Of the hospital, called the Rum Hospital, built from the proceeds of a tax on spirits, Hannibal is very scathing. 'In addition to building the hospital, the public are to fill the pockets of the Contractors and what crowns the concern is that there are no sick to occupy it and it is generally thought sufficiently large for a general hospital to the West Indies, besides affording Palaces for the Surgeon and Staff . . .' Mary Macarthur was later to marry the chief surgeon and live in the palace.

In 1813 Mrs Macarthur built a new large woolshed and was very much exercised in her mind over washing the wool, which was washed on the sheep's back three days before shearing, but still Macarthur complained that it arrived in London very dirty. That year she had one thousand, three hundred ewes in lamb. The winter was a severe one, frosty and dry, so that there was no grass and cattle starved. There was a wheat shortage and the price rose to one pound a bushel. The summer came in burning hot, and the crops withered. Mrs Macarthur had some anxious months, but the drought broke in February 1814, and by May conditions were good and prospects fair, but there were other worries. The natives had become troublesome. Hannibal Macarthur wrote to his uncle, 'We have become sufferers in the Death of a shepherd's wife and your old favourite, Wm Baker, who were inhumanly murdered at the Upper Camden yards. This horrid event was represented to the Governor but he is so much taken up with a parade of the garrison that he has 'no means of defence or protection for those distant establishments', so that the possession of stock is rendered very precarious as, in addition to the natives, numbers of convicts are roving uncontrolled through the country committing all kinds of depredations, and, I have every reason to believe, some of them were concerned with the natives in the attack on our yards.' The occurrence was repeated two years later, and again two lives were lost. This was very harassing, especially for the victims. Elizabeth Farm itself was never in danger.

The summer of 1814–15 was again very dry and the wheat harvest failed. 1815 was an even more anxious time for the stock suffered severely, only about half the lambs born being reared. Thinking of the cares thus inflicted on her, her husband wrote: 'It will be the study of my life to requite you for all that you have suffered on my account.' But there were compensations which he also recognized when he wrote: 'Yet it is some consolation when I reflect that you must also experience many gratifying moments at the success of your exertions to supply my place and to perform those duties that my present fate denies me the power of executing myself . . .' She was a woman happy in the full exercise of her considerable faculties. These were her great years. She did not merely carry out her husband's instructions, she was herself an innovator. She was the first to make hay and sell it, the first to extract stumps when she cleared land. Macquarie granted her six hundred acres of land in the Parramatta district as an acknowledgement of her services to the community in progressive agriculture and sheep-raising. Her life was cast in pleasant places and in the midst of plenty. A letter to Miss Kingdon in March 1816 portrays its bountiful aspect:

'I know not what I can say of our mode of life that will give you a correct idea of it. It is a mixture of town and country life; and yet, in many respects, unlike anything you can have experienced. Our climate is delightful and we have in high perfection and in great abundance the fruits of warm and cold countries. In our garden, which is large, we have Oranges, Lemons, Olives, Almonds, Grapes, Peaches, Apricots, Nectarines, Medlars, Pears, Apples, Raspberries, Strawberries, Walnuts, Cherries, Plums. These fruits you know. Then we have the Loquat, a Chinese fruit, the Citron, the Shaddock and the Pomegranate . . . We have an abundance, even to profusion, in so much that our Pigs are fed on Peaches, Apricots and Melons in the season . . . We grow wheat, barley, oats, we make hay, at least I do, and so does Mrs Macquarie, but the practice is not general; we feed hogs, we have cattle, keep a dairy, fatten beef and mutton and export fine wool.'

The fullness of life was hers. She had access to whatever society there was, and she had her finger, as it were, on the growing point of a nation. Everywhere about her new life and purpose were springing up. Sydney was now a busy port. 'At this time,' she wrote in 1816, 'we have a vessel in the harbour from America, two from Bengal, one from Canton, one from the Cape, and one from Ceylon; one also from the Isle of France, several from Europe, which are about to depart by way of Java, China, or India.' Perhaps she remembered the starving Sydney and empty harbour of her first arrival as she wrote.


*IV*
*The Family Group*

There may have been a shade of anti-climax in Macarthur's long desired return. In England he looked upon Australia as a peaceful paradise where he would recover tranquillity of mind and health of body. But, alas, he brought back with him his proud temper and his ailments. The very moment of his arrival was marred by an attack of flying gout. In the years that followed he was often a prey to deep depression, based not on circumstance, which continued to smile, but on his physical state. Everything looked black. 'My feeble attempt to introduce merino sheep still creeps on almost unheeded and altogether unassisted,' he wrote to his friend Walter Davidson in 1818.

There must have been readjustments that were not always painless. Macarthur was not the man to leave management to his wife, however highly he rated her capabilities, when he was himself on the spot. It cannot have been altogether easy to surrender the reins. There is a change in Mrs Macarthur's letters. The accent falls more strongly on social occasions, and the two boys, James and William, who returned with their father, bulk very large in her correspondence. We hear of riding and shooting parties, entertainments for the officers of the garrison and their wives (if any), visitors from India and China come to Sydney to recuperate, the amusing novelty of some Maoris from New Zealand. The family became a group, a close-knit partnership, working with all its energy to round out the family estate and further the wool industry. John, in England, acted as his father's agent and trained his mind on the legal problems of the wool industry, moving for lowered tariffs and government assistance. He also bought and shipped household supplies for his mother. We find her writing to him for 'blue cloth for servants' Liveries . . . about 20/- a yard and the gross of large and gross of small yellow buttons with our crest'; for household linen and clothes which 'should be of good quality, both because they are better taken care of, are in the end more useful, certainly more respectable, and in the object of package and freight cost no more than trash . . . The last cambric muslins we were greatly deceived in. Your sister made them up into dresses; they washed to pieces immediately – injured, we suppose, in the bleaching'.

The Camden property was turned over to James and William with, as their agricultural mentor, the gardener, Andrew Murray, who had been with Sir Walter Scott at Abbotsford. The only complaints their father had of them were that they had not 'sufficient hardness of character to manage the people placed under their control, and they set too little value upon money'. The girls helped their mother and showed no wish to marry. 'They are too sensitive and too well-principled for this society,' wrote their father. Later Mary and Emmeline both married, but Elizabeth, who was very delicate, did not.

Macarthur was now withdrawn from public affairs. He got on well with Macquarie and was *persona grata* with Commissioner Bigge, who was sent out at the end of Macquarie's governorship to investigate the affairs of the colony. He lent him horses and talked land grants. With Sir Thomas and Lady Brisbane the Macarthurs were very friendly until an unfortunate occurrence. Brisbane offered Macarthur a magistracy, but on instructions from England the appointment was withdrawn. Macarthur was furious and tried to challenge Judge Barron Field to a duel, but that gentleman remained entrenched behind his office. To placate him, Brisbane offered magistracies to his sons, James and William, who indignantly refused the honour. At these times Mrs Macarthur seems to have retreated into the woman's prerogative of that day of not understanding and therefore not being compelled to notice men's affairs. Her friendship with Lady Brisbane and her sister was untouched. 'The ladies,' she wrote to Miss Kingdon, 'are fond of and live in great retirement. They mix little in society and give none of those large entertainments which Mrs Macquarie used to do. They have a Dinner Party once a week. Their table is handsomely set out and served in a manner superior to anything we have yet seen in the colony. Lady Brisbane has a good Piano on which she occasionally plays and accompanies the instrument with her voice. Mrs Macdougall plays the harp and Mr Runiker the piano in turn.' Elizabeth's memories are lengthening. Did she think in these genteel days of Mr Worgan's piano and the dashing young officers of her first years in Australia?

The family was going from strength to strength. In 1822 Macarthur received the second grant of five thousand acres promised him by Lord Camden. In 1823, by lease, exchange and grant, he increased his property by more than twelve thousand acres. In 1822 and 1824 he was honoured by the Society of Arts in London and received gold medals for his wool. In 1824, too, Edward, the eldest son, came home for ten months, and Mary married Dr Bowman. Macarthur now had an establishment of eighty convict servants, who received a weekly ration of seven pounds of beef or mutton, a peck of wheat, vegetables, milk, fruit, tea and sugar, clothing as required, some tobacco and a money payment of fifteen pounds a year, to which he added bonuses of from one pound to five pounds for good conduct. Unruly servants were reduced to the government wage of ten pounds a year. Many of these men were employed as shepherds, for the sheep were then treated in the English style. Each shepherd had a maximum flock of five hundred sheep, generally smaller, and folded them at night. At the beginning of this decade Macarthur had six thousand, eight hundred sheep, of which three hundred were pure-bred merinos. He was getting up to twenty-eight pounds for his rams. He conceived the idea, fortunate both for himself and for the country, of selling rams to the government for breeding in Tasmania and taking payment in land at the rate of seven and six an acre. This plan, a little modified, was carried out and greatly increased his estate. In 1828 his wool was bringing from five shillings to seven and six a pound. The wool business was very intricate owing to the distance from the European market and the effect of the long sea voyage on the wool.

The troubles and struggles of the outer world only reached Mrs Macarthur dimly thorugh all this thick wadding of felicity. In her letters we hear now of a plague of bushrangers, who fell on outlying farms at dusk, 'destroying and carrying off all' – but not on Macarthur's property; of natives giving trouble at Bathurst and of 'our present greatest annoyance . . . from a licentious Press'. Sturt's discoveries leave faint echoes, and Mrs Macarthur notes with approval 'the number of respectable persons who begin to arrive from England is now considerable'.

Elizabeth was growing old placidly, and her husband was growing querulously old. After many years she was homesick for England but knew that she would never see it again. She wrote to her son Edward: 'Well, indeed, do I remember the East Park, the old vicarage house, its aspect towards the sea, from whence rude gusts would frequently shake and assail the apartments above more especially. These scenes of my childhood and youth cannot be easily forgotten, nor will the memory of dear friends departed, nor of those who still remain, once my young playfellows, be effaced from my memory while it pleases God that I retain that faculty. Mr Kingdon forgets my age when he speaks of my return to my still dear native land. The time is too far past.' That was in 1830; she had twenty more years to live. Her sight was no longer good. 'I cannot even read over to correct what I have written.' 'I cannot see to round a pen,' but Edward sent her some newfangled steel nibs. She was still a happy woman. Her garden was her delight. She was tranquil and fulfilled. There is a portrait of her done at about this time, a handsome, resolute old lady in a black taffeta dress and a rust-coloured scarf, at peace with the world and full of calm strength.

One of her latest letters to be preserved is addressed to her eldest son and dated from Woolloomooloo (spelt 'Woolloomullah. What a name!'), where her youngest daughter, now Mrs Watson, lived. It describes a saunter through the Botanic Gardens, and they immediately take on the air of a private park. 'We walked in the Botanic Gardens together with Mary and Mr B. I believe we sauntered about three hours or more, looked at many things you had contributed to the collection, and among the number the Arbutus – it had grown out of my knowledge; it is just now breaking into flower.'

In 1834 John Macarthur died at Camden. His wife hoped till the end that he would 'gradually become less visionary', but he carried his 'restlessness' up to the edge of the grave. He was buried on a spot chosen by himself, a hill with a wide view over the cowpastures, his property, its flocks and its herds.

The remainder of Mrs Macarthur's life appears to have been untroubled and quiet, its only tragedy her eldest daughter's death some ten years after her husband's. She died in 1850 and was buried beside her husband at Camden Park. Her life covered the first great pastoral period in Australian history, from its beginning in those Bengal ewes, more like goats than sheep, to its waning just before the discovery of gold. She died on the threshold of a new era.

# DORA WILCOX

## Jenny *

Her portrait hung upon a wall
Of the old home, and watched us all
Laughing, as she, the pioneer,
Had laughed through many a troubled year
In a new land to which she came
With her true love. We knew her name
Was Jenny.
        So when first with feet
Of flesh I trod a Bristol street,
Dreaming I went. Had Destiny
Patterned the stuff of life for me?
Or was it Chance now interweaving
Threads of past joy with present grieving?
For in that city of the west,
Where lay my soldier-son at rest,
Jenny was born in days gone by;
Not then in alien earth, thought I,
He sleeps.
        I stood where she had stood
Long, long ago; the April flood
Of green in blade and leaf and bud
Had swept the woodlands, winter-bleak,
Triumphantly that Easter-week,
But I who heard the blackbirds sing
Saw through my tears the English spring.

---

*In Arno's Vale Cemetery, near Bristol, England, several Australian soldiers who died in hospital are buried. For many years after the Great War it was the custom to lay primroses upon the graves on Anzac Day.

Yet mellow in the morning glow
Looked the old city spread below
To me, who high on Brandon Hill
Wandered; and do the young folk still
Steal out across the river now
To meet, and kiss, beneath the bough
In the white moonlight, as those two
Lovers long dead were used to do?
Ah, yes! for spring processional passes
With other lads and other lasses,
And the green trysting-tree lives on,
Though Jenny and her lad are gone.

Are gone! but something of them clung –
Something lighthearted, and as young
As my dear son – to Bristol yet;
Only the dead whom we forget
Are lost to life.
            By bridge I went,
By house, and wall, and monument
Unchanged since Jenny took one day,
For the last time, the self-same way.
And as her image with persistence
Lived in my mind – thus all existence
Is doubled – I was not alone
In the great church of carven stone,
Saint Mary Redcliffe. Tripping in,
Defiant of her cautious kin,
Came Jenny in a muslin gown,
With rosy cheeks and curls of brown
As in her picture. Where she made
Her vow, I saw her, unafraid
Of the new life, the unknown land,
Smile, as her husband took her hand
In his.
      To them, we know, ungracious
Seemed the far country, and the spacious
Unpeopled bushland; harsh the cries
Of unfamiliar birds – the skies
Too hard, too blinding to their eyes
In the fierce heat of summer. Yet

Jenny endured, and lived to set
Lilac and lavender and heart's-ease
In her new garden overseas.

And I? In Arno's Vale I found
Among the Australian graves a mound
Primrose-strewn – for an Anzac Day
The Pilgrims come each year to lay
Fresh garlands – but I saw them not,
Nor the calm loveliness of the spot.
I was not there. The sunlight streaming
Fell on the orange-orchards gleaming
Along the patterned hill again.
Dotted with sheep, the endless plain
Stretched into blue infinity
Where lay the wheat, like yellow sea,
Vineyards, and farms, and homes of men.
Against the Australian landscape then –
Hostile to English eyes, but grown
Dear and familiar to our own –
I saw his face, so full of light
That I was dazzled. Was my sight
Confused? Was Jenny, or my son,
Before me? Surely they were one
In spirit?
          The old days are gone,
Days of slow journeyings and dearth.
Another age is ours; the earth
Yields in abundance, and afar
And shadowy, seems the nightmare, War.
So much is done! – so much is left
To do! Imperfect is the weft
Of national life; the manifold
New threads, replacing now the old
And worn, we cannot yet combine
Into fresh beauty of design.

O pioneers, O son of mine!
Though the world changes and we turn
This way and that, and no stars burn
In empty heaven to point the way,

Your Lamp of Courage casts a ray,
Cutting a dark, a beacon-flame.
Soldiers who went, and you who came
To found for us material good,
How shall we build a brotherhood?
How clear our land of selfish greed
And sloth? Your purposeful will we need
In this, the spiritual war we wage
To make, and keep, our heritage
Happier than in the bygone years,
O son of mine! O pioneers!

# DYMPHNA CUSACK

## Mary Reibey and her Times

### I

On 7 October 1792, an East Indiaman, the *Royal Admiral*, sailed into Sydney Harbour, seventeen weeks out from England. We have no record of the feelings of the three hundred and forty-eight convicts aboard as they approached the country that, for the majority, must be their prison and their home for the rest of their lives. Even those whose terms of transportation were relatively short had little hope of ever leaving it. According to Lord Sydney, secretary of state for the Home Department, 'the remoteness of its situation, from which it is hardly possible for persons to return without permission', rendered the thought of a penal settlement in New South Wales peculiarly pleasing. And, indeed, since the refusal of the American colonies to take English convicts, the government found itself in a serious quandary. In its vain efforts to cope with the results of a harsh and brutalizing penal code, which sought equally vainly to discourage the evils arising from an unjust and brutal social system, its policy went no deeper than the mere disposal of its victims. The fact that, in nineteenth-century England, there were over two hundred capital offences and a far larger number punishable with transportation and that they ranged from murder and mutiny to horse-stealing, poaching and democratic principles, makes it remarkable that the country was not entirely depopulated of its enterprising citizens.

However bitter the despair that gripped the hearts of the exiles on the *Royal Admiral* as they gazed on the unfamiliar scene, it must have been mitigated in some measure by the thought that they would, at least, be freed from the horrors of their 'floating hell'.

The *Royal Admiral* was more over-crowded than any of the

ships of the First Fleet, of which Governor Phillip had complained so strongly. In spite of the fact that they were well attended to by the ship's surgeon and officers a fever broke out among the convicts; ten died and eighty-eight were on the sick list when the ship arrived. The forty-seven females were more fortunate than the majority of women convicts of whom Phillip wrote: 'The conditions of their transportation stamp the magistrates with infamy.' The fact that none of them perished was attributed to the greater freedom and more liberal diet they had.

To eyes accustomed to duller English skies, and weakened by long confinement, the clearness of that spring morning in Sydney must have seemed intolerably alien; the intricate wooded hills running down to water's edge, sombre and menacing. Its wildness held no beauty for those whose hearts turned passionately to quiet English villages set among ordered fields; and to those who had been born and bred in crowded city streets, its vastness was little short of terrifying. At night strange stars blazed overhead, remote and comfortless, and the incredible blue of the ocean was to them only a tangible seal on their exile.

The diary of George Thompson, one of the gunners on the ship, gives some interesting facts about the convicts they carried.

'There are four boys on board, fifteen years old, transported for seven years; one of nineteen, transported for life. Three girls, Ann Wilson, eighteen, Ann Holmes, only sixteen, and "— Scott", only fifteen years of age, transported for life.'

'— Scott' cloaks the identity of the girl whose life for the next sixty-three years was to move against the stirring pageant of Australian progress, whose fortunes were as varied and whose achievements as remarkable as those of the colony she came to regard as her 'country'.

What mixed emotions woke in Mary Haydock (alias Scott), fifteen-year-old 'criminal', whose sentence of death for the heinous offence of riding a neighbour's horse in a madcap escapade when she was only thirteen had been 'mercifully commuted' to transportation! [The horse-riding incident has frequently caused Mary Reibey to be confused with Margaret Catchpole. Apart from many other differences, Margaret Catchpole did not reach the colony till 1801 and died in 1819.]

At fifteen, two years of imprisonment, with all the anguish of disgrace, the physical misery of prison life, the anger of her respectable Lancashire family – who had her sent out under an assumed name – must provide an almost unbridgeable gap. *Her* thoughts were turned to the future, not to the past.

To Mary Haydock, if to none of the other convicts, New South Wales spelled freedom and life. Whatever regrets she had for her old life were swept away in the excitement of the new; whatever fears the new might have held were quietened by the knowledge that she was not facing it alone. Thomas Raby, twenty-five-year-old officer on the *Royal Admiral*, defying the traditions of the old English family to which he belonged, and the prestige of the East India Service, had asked her to be his wife. It says much for his force of character and independence of mind that he dared take a step so unconventional that his fellow officers regarded him as nothing but a quixotic young fool.

It says much for the charm of Mary's personality, too, that he should be prepared to make the many sacrifices involved in marrying her: It meant giving up the service for which he had been trained – and the East India Service ranked next to the navy; sacrificing his family relationships, his prospects; and starting life anew in a new world with a wife who, whatever her personal charm and innocence, must always bear the stigma of convictism.

Yet, to both of them, as they watched the water whipped to blue and silver in the open harbour, and deepening to rich secret greens in the sheltered bays, the crude settlement seemed the very home of adventure and romance. The wind, full of a strange tangy scent entirely unknown to them, tossed Mary's dark curls about her young face and set her wide brown eyes dancing. Beginning in misery and defeat, the voyage was ending in joy and hope. Any scruples Thomas Raby might have had on the wisdom of his decision were stilled. He had no illusions about the difficulties ahead, but he was young and very much in love. Besides, there was strength in that young mouth, with its upturned corners, and in the chin too firmly rounded for beauty, and not even the first glimpse of the primitive township could discourage him.

Primitive it certainly was. The Sydney wharfage consisted of natural rocks; the streets, called 'rows', were thickly studded with stumps of trees and consisted of bark huts, of which there were about five hundred in all. Rocky headlands covered with thick timber surrounded the little township and Woolloomooloo was considered to be in the country.

The usual procedure for the disposal of convicts was that, on arrival of the transports, the government claimed those whose trade or profession in happier days had made them desirable; the officers of the New South Wales Corps had the second choice, and the rest were divided among the civilians. It was Phillip's policy that 'the few women who still retain some degree of virtue should be kept together', but the fact that Mary was betrothed to a free settler put her in still another category.

Governor Phillip, always sympathetic to the unfortunates in his charge, arranged that Thomas Raby should be responsible for the care of Mary Haydock till they were ready to marry and thus she escaped the worst features of life in the colony from the point of view of a woman convict. The young couple often discussed plans for their life together as they walked by the rivulet that suppled the settlement with water. Descending from marshy ground near where Hyde Park stands today, it ran in a beautiful creek of fresh water, fringed with heavy timber, to Bridge Street, being fed by two good streams – one at King Street and another at Spring Street. In May 1792, a tank of solid rock was constructed along its course to hold eight thousand gallons of water, and from this it got its name.

Phillip, worn out by a long and incessant struggle with the stupidity of officialdom, the poor quality of the material with which he had to work, and the barrenness of a country that had apparently no natural resources for the sustenance of the five thousand persons for whom he was responsible, was still optimistic, and sufficiently farsighted to announce in the midst of a recital of the colony's troubles: 'Nor do I doubt but that this country will prove the most valuable acquisition Great Britain ever made.'

Till his departure in December 1792, the government alone was permitted to trade, but during the three years of the lieutenant-governorship of Major Grose and Captain Paterson the commercial administration of the colony underwent a great change. The 102nd Regiment might have been blind to their duties in the settlement, but they were not blind to their own profit.

Thomas Raby was the first free settler to trade outside the military ring, a privilege no doubt secured by his previous connection with the East India Service. He made his first start in his new life with an investment he had intended for the Indian trade. The regulations of the East Indian Service permitted their officers to speculate in the ports, and as a further concession they could carry goods free of charge in quantities proportionate to their rank. Raby sold his investment and since the usual profits made in New South Wales ranged from 100 per cent to 500 per cent, he no doubt did very well. Till 1798 only government officials, including the military, were allowed to retail goods. Phillip had wisely decreed that no liquor was to be brought into the colony, but in the years that elapsed between his departure and Hunter's arrival in 1795 it became the most profitable article of trade. 'Rum was the universal barter,' John Macarthur said, and it was from the enormous profits made on it that the corps received its significant and unflattering nickname of the 'Rum Corps'.

Officers only could buy from the king's stores. They bought at cost price and retailed to soldiers and settlers at enormous profit. When a new cargo arrived, they apportioned it among themselves. Settlers were victimized by the clique, which forced them to sell at fixed prices produce, which was in turn sold to the government stores at prices assessed by the military. 'In 1797,' said Margarot, one of the Scotch 'martyrs', 'a combination bond was entered into by the officers, by which they were neither to underbuy nor undersell the one from the other.'

Within two years Raby had established himself as one of Sydney's traders; he had also obtained a farm on the Hawkesbury, so he then approached Major Grose, who gave him permission to marry Mary Haydock and granted her a pardon. On 7 September 1794, they were married in the first St Phillip's – a wattle and daub church situated where Hunter and Bligh streets join today.

A crisp morning in early spring; the pungent scent of bush flowers drifting into the church; the carolling of magpies and the clank of chains as road gangs went by; curious eyes turned on the young couple as they made their way over the rough road, women convicts watching with envy the consummation of a romance that must have seemed like a fairytale to them; Mary radiant in an Indian muslin frock Thomas had secured in one of his cargoes, her dark curls clustering around her wide, high forehead, her merry brown eyes more sober than usual under their exquisitely arched brows. No doubt she was not the only one who was envied in that community where women were so scarce.

## II

The first years of their married life were spent at the farm on the Hawkesbury and here, in 1796, their first son was born. But Raby was no farmer; he was a sailor and a trader; the sea was in his blood, so the farm was leased and he came to Sydney and engaged in mercantile pursuits. Following the popular example set by the military, he also acquired a number of farms held as security for goods sold, though, contrary to the usual custom, there is no suggestion that he employed any but the legitimate commercial methods of the day.

The Rabys opened a store, which their association with the East India Company enabled them to stock easily. Mary's business acumen and education enabled her to take an active part in its management, while her husband went about the country and attended to rural business. Thus, from her earliest days, she watched at close hand the development of the great proprietorial fortunes of the colony, begun for the most part in fraud and extortion and developed in brutality and oppression. With her keen powers of observation she was not slow to realize that the accumulation of private fortunes rarely played a part in the constructive development of the colony from a penal settlement. Whatever benefit accrued was by accident rather than by design. Governor Hunter showed some slight scepticism about John Macarthur's professed public spirit when he suggested taking convicts 'off the government's hands' and paying them a bread rate of fivepence a day instead of the current rate of five shillings, just as Bligh, a little later, not unnaturally refused to regard his desire to extend the wool industry as due to pure benevolence.

While Mrs Raby looked after the store and minded her growing family, her husband, in partnership with Edward Wills, bought a small sloop, the *Raven*, and engaged in seal fishing. The voyage of Matthew Flinders in the *Norfolk* in 1798 had revealed the possibilities for sealing in Furneaux and adjacent islands in the Straits, and Governor King encouraged 'the pursuit as much as possible to those who may be of industrious and enterprising dispositions among the inhabitants'.

These were turbulent days in the colony. Provisions were scarce and expensive; the fertile farms suffered greatly from floods; the evil effects of the rum traffic were visible everywhere; the military clique daily increased its power, and its insolence and disregard of duty made discipline so difficult to maintain in the area already occupied, consisting of a narrow strip along the Hawkesbury, a section running east and west along the Parramatta, and a strip connecting the two, that both Hunter and King were reluctant to encourage further inland exploration.

A few prosperous years enabled the Rabys, who in the meantime had for some unknown reason altered the spelling of their name [Thomas Raby used Reiby, Reibie and Reibey but the signature on his will was Reibey and after his death his wife and children adopted that form] to build a residence and warehouse combined. Thomas was frequently absent sealing, carrying coal and timber to Newcastle, and, later, trading in the islands, so the bulk of the business fell on Mary. The lower storey of Entally House, as Thomas called the stone building, which formed one of the most conspicuous landmarks at the head of the cove, was used as a warehouse. In the spacious upper rooms the growing family lived – there were now five children – and from the attic windows the Reibey boys watched every ship that came into the cove, when they were not playing 'French and English' in the scrub on Benelong Point, or envying the red-coated sentry on the governor's jetty.

Their extensive waterfront adjoined the government wharf and faced the open area that in 1810 was named Macquarie Place. All the traffic from the wharf ran past the house, and a motley crowd of Lascars, full-blooded Tahitians and Maoris, left stranded by unscrupulous ship-owners, jostled around the wharf waiting for ships. Foreign-looking sailors carrying richly plumaged birds, which they hoped to exchange for something more useful, haunted the building. Within, the low substantial rooms, crowded with incongruous and exotic stores, were redolent of sandalwood. From the windows could be seen the lawns and shrubberies of Government House, running right down to the water's edge, and the three windmills that crowned the crest of the hill on which it was built made changing patterns against the sky.

Busily occupied with the receipt of cargoes, the sale and despatch of goods, advertisements in the *Sydney Gazette* and the thousand details of a large warehouse, Mary still found time to teach her children their letters. Several assigned women helped her with the household tasks, and on one of his voyages to the islands, Thomas brought back an Otaheitean girl as a present to his wife. 'Fee Foo' became nursemaid to the children, and the affection with which she was regarded by them all was revealed by the extensive enquiries set on foot for her recovery when she disappeared in 1813.

Sydney provided some extraordinary contrasts in the early days of the nineteenth century. To the extremely varied convict population had been added political prisoners, who naturally refused to be treated as ordinary criminals. Irish rebels sent out for participation in the rebellion of 1798; the Scotch 'martyrs': men of enlightened political opinions and high personal integrity like Skirving; Dr Redfern, transported for being suspected of sympathising with the mutineers on the *Nore*.

The rum traffic, while enriching the military and free traders, impoverished and debauched free settlers and convicts alike. In his proclamation in February 1807 Governor Bligh 'laments to find by his late visit through the colony that the most calamitous evils were rife, and feels it his duty to put a total stop to this barter in future'.

Throughout these tumultuous years the Reibeys occupied themselves with the expansion of their trading activities. The shortage of meat induced Thomas to build a schooner for the island trade, and the fact that the vessel was on the stocks for nearly eighteen months shows the deplorable lack of even the commonest materials in the colony. It was at last launched, christened the *Mercury*, and sailed in December 1807 for the islands, with a cargo for barter and a large quantity of salt for curing pigs.

The colony was seething with unrest. Labour was so dear that Macarthur was supported by all the big landowners when he opposed the suggestion that emancipated convicts should be given small farms, insisting that these 'idle, worthless poor . . . should be obliged to employ themselves in the service of honest and vigilant masters'. That masters vigilant of their own interests were not hard to find was proved by the fact that in 1808 the Rum Corps cornered the provision market, and prices soared to two and six a pound for flour and meal, and five shillings for a two pound loaf. Tea was selling at six shillings an ounce, sugar at four shillings a pound, butter six shillings a pound, tobacco twenty-four shillings a pound, coarse white calico five shillings a yard. In a letter written about this time, Margaret Catchpole complains that she had to pay 'fifteen shillings for a pr of Black Spanish shoses and the same for a par of cotten stockenes'.

Bligh, faced with a difficult and unprecedented situation, behaved in a high-handed and overbearing fashion. His efforts to check 'the calamitous evils', of which he had spoken earlier, made him increasingly unpopular with the trading and military classes. The Reibeys, astute business people that they were, kept themselves entirely clear of the quarrels between the governor and the insurgents.

The Reibeys were wearied of their constant separations, and Thomas applied for the position of pilot in Sydney Harbour. His appointment in 1809 was proof of his skill as well as of his popularity with the governor. But apparently the peaceful routine of a pilot's life did not suit him, and, in October 1810, he set out on a last voyage to India. He took thirty-five tons of sandalwood, which he sold at Whampoa, and then proceeded to Calcutta, where he was very ill of sunstroke. An advertisement in the *Sydney Gazette* on his return presents such an extraordinary variety of articles for sale that the Reibeys might be called the first 'universal providers'. It also indicates an astonishingly luxurious standard of living in a penal settlement, where common articles of use were still very scarce among the poorer classes.

Reibey's warehouse presented for sale, 'Teas of sorts, sugar and sugar-candy, rice and coffee, salt and saltpetre, spices and pepper, bacon, pork and beef, hog's cheeks, lard, sausages, calicoes, nankeens, ready-made shirts, chemises, satins of sorts, black silks, silk handkerchiefs of sorts, velvet waistcoats, China hats, sewing silk of colours, sash, ribbands, black ribband, tortoiseshell combs, ivory tea-chests, lacquered ditto, metal buttons, lacquered waiters, gilt looking-glasses, walking-sticks, beads, long sets of china, short breakfast ditto, flat plates, hotwater ditto, chamber vessels, wash-hand basons, goblets, large teapots, lge. tureens compleat, curry ditto, sugar and cream pots, punch bowls, pint basons, mugs in sets, cups and saucers, china, paper and a variety of other articles.'

Just what profit such a cargo yielded it is impossible to say exactly, but it must have been very high, for Macquarie's restrictive regulations applied only to provisions. He made it an indictable offence to act as a middleman in the sale of produce except under special restrictions. As a result prices, while still very high, dropped considerably.

Thomas Reibey never fully recovered from his sunstroke in Calcutta, and after an illness of six months, died at Entally House, in May 1811. The long partnership between Mary Haydock and

Thomas Reibey was dissolved. Whatever he had sacrificed for the young convict girl had been more than repaid. Their life in the colony had been arduous, but it had been successful to a degree that the young officer on the *Royal Admiral* had never dreamed. In his nineteen years in the colony he had certainly founded a fortune. But he had done far more than that: he had founded a family, and for over a century and more the name of Reibey was synonymous with dignified and honourable service in the country he had, by so strange a turn of fortune, made his own. [With the death of the Hon. Thomas Reibey in Tasmania, in 1912, went the last of the name in Australia.]

The potentialities he had divined in his young bride had developed to a degree that made theirs a marriage rare in any time, and especially so in the nineteenth century. It was a real partnership, and their mutual affection and trust deepened with the years. It was a saddened family that gathered to take their last leave of the man whose proud and adventurous spirit had encouraged and inspired them: Thomas was only fifteen, spirited and venturesome like his father; James still younger; George, at twelve, already the book-lover and the scholar, sensitive to the brutality and misery around him; Celia, at ten, showing promise of a delicate beauty; and three young daughters, Eliza, Jane Penelope and Elizabeth Anne. Mary herself, comforting her children, distraught with business worries, through all the confusion and the weeping remained dignified and capable. For her there was no relief in easy tears; her loss was too deep for that. Leaden-hearted, she watched the long procession move to the cemetery in George Street, and as in a dream all the happiness and the hardships, the struggles and achievements of those crowded seventeen years passed before her.

Her husband's remains were removed later to the new cemetery at the Sandhills and placed in a bricked-in vault with an altar tomb, where they lay till the cemeteries were resumed for the railway station. The inscription on the tomb was very simple: 'Sacred to the memory of Mr Thomas Reiby, who departed this life on 5th May, 1811. Aged 42 years.'

## III

The death of Edward Wills in the same month as her husband left Mary with entire control of the business, and letters of administration were taken out in her name. She had seven children, the eldest of them barely fifteen; she was an emancipist, whose social position was no longer secured by the presence of her 'free' husband. But she was not deterred by any of these handicaps, and launched out into an entirely new venture by moving from the large stone house in Macquarie Place to No. 12 George Street. There she inaugurated radical reforms in the retail trade, which no doubt were as unpopular with her competitors as they were popular with all classes of buyers.

She announced by advertisement that she 'has laid in a variety of articles recently imported in the *Providence*, which she is determined to sell at reasonable prices, assuring herself it is the best recommendation to public patronage and support'. Just what 'reasonable prices' were we do not know, but Margaret Catchpole reported in 1812: 'Everything very deear, butter five shillens par lb.'

She was also engaged in the wine and spirit trade, for in 1810 Thomas Reibey appeared on the list of one of the twenty registered hotel-keepers.

The year after her husband's death she made her first application for a grant of land. Macquarie, with whom she was a great favourite, granted her request for two hundred acres at Airds, near Camden. She might have asked for two thousand, but she had no intention of going in for farming on a large scale, and Macquarie had wisely put a stop to land speculation by forbidding the sale of grants within five years. Besides, she had several of the best farms on the Hawkesbury, which she let to tenants who paid a good rent.

Her eldest son, Thomas, who had made several voyages with his father, was for two or three years a pupil at Rev. Halloran's Classical, Mathematical and Commercial Academy in Hunter Street, but his taste was for the sea.

Conditions were changing rapidly in the colony. Governor Macquarie's appointment was the beginning of a new system of administration, for his policy that 'this country should be made the home, and the happy home, to every emancipated convict who deserves it' was little short of revolutionary.

His attempts to promote friendly relations between emancipists and free settlers failed, for the most prominent of the free men were either ex-officers of the New South Wales Corps or else men who had sided with them against Bligh, and they would have no truck with 'these men wanting in moral principle', as the Rev. Samuel Marsden called them, speaking, it must be felt, rather as a wealthy settler, with an eye to the main chance, than a minister of God. They had no objections to trading with them for their own benefit, but it was a far cry from commercial advantage to civic rights, and the 'Exclusives' were determined that no ex-convict, whatever his merits, should enjoy the rights of a citizen while they could prevent it.

Mary Reibey was deeply interested in the problems that faced the governor, for her diary contains many closely written pages copied from Bigge's report upon Macquarie's administration in 1818. A woman who found time to make copies of evidence, and still carry on all the duties she had, is little short of remarkable. Though we have no definite record of the part she played in the granting of civil rights to emancipists, her excellent qualities, in common with those of Dr Redfern, the Rev. Fulton, and others, must certainly have helped to convince the governor of the soundness of his policy.

She was no doubt far too busy to take any part in the social activities of the colony, in spite of her taste for them. And, indeed, the peculiar circumstances of her situation would have made it difficult. Because of her early escapade she was debarred from the society of those women with whom she would naturally have associated by reason of her origin and her education, and on the other hand she could have nothing in common with the majority of the poor wretches who were sent out under similar circumstances.

Each year her business was increasing, and she began to launch out into ship-owning. Following the wreck of the *Mercury* at Shoalhaven in 1813, she bought the *John Palmer* for trade with Van Diemen's Land. As other Sydney merchants joined in, the island farmers complained bitterly that they were being shamefully exploited by the Sydney traders, who bought grain at a dollar a bushel, or less, paying growers in stores at exorbitant prices, and selling in Sydney at ten to twenty shillings a bushel. The dangers of the coastal trade were very great and losses of ship-owners correspondingly high. There is no doubt that all the owners, without exception, tried to minimize their possible losses by the age-old methods of those who get someone else to go down to the sea in ships for them. Cheap vessels were built; they were poorly provisioned, and badly manned with assigned convicts,

Lascars and islanders at deplorably low rates. Shrewd and occasionally ruthless Mary might have grown with years of battling against the unscrupulous methods of early Sydney, but she was generous as well. When Matthews, with his wife, their two children and two other men were wrecked about two hundred miles north of Sydney, they walked back along the coast, and after appalling difficulties reached Newcastle; Thomas Reibey gave them passages back to Sydney, and on their arrival Mary took them into her care and collected enough money in a day to give them a new start.

In 1817 she bought the brig *Gov. Macquarie* for the low price of seven hundred and fifty pounds. Tom sometimes commanded her, but his mother had determined to set him up in Van Diemen's Land as a land-owner and merchant. Accordingly, after his marriage with Richarda Allen, a daughter of the medical attendant of George IV, they sailed in the *Gov. Macquarie* to Hobart Town, carrying a cargo as miscellaneous as that his father had brought back from India, which he advertised for sale at 'very reduced prices, for ready money'.

With the successful settlement of her son in Van Diemen's Land, she sat back with a sigh of relief, and determined to enjoy a little leisure. The momentous decision of going for a trip to England had been made as early as 1816, when she advertised all her property for sale. The list included 'a valuable and extensive dwelling – a house with large stores of water, in George St. A valuable house and premises in Macquarie Place, seven large farms on the Hawkesbury, all most productive and valuable', and a 'house and premises in Cockle Bay'. In all, she was estimated to be worth twenty thousand pounds, all accumulated in twenty years. For many years the Bank of New South Wales rented the premises in Macquarie Place at one hundred and fifty pounds a year, and carried on their business there. Later the Church and School Corporation occupied it, and, in 1837, when the business of the Colonial Revenue Department was consolidated with the Treasurer's Department, they occupied the building at a rental of two hundred and fifty pounds a year.

The struggle between 'Exclusives' and emancipists was at its height when Mrs Reibey sailed for England in 1820, accompanied by her two daughters Celia and Eliza; Macquarie, the last of the autocrats, was approaching the end of his term as governor, and the 'Exclusives' hoped that Bigge's strictures on his policy would lead to fundamental changes when his successor arrived.

## IV

It must have been with very mixed feelings that Mary Reibey landed in England in June 1820. It was nearly twenty-nine years since she had left, degraded and outcast. Now she had returned a wealthy widow of forty-three, with two attractive daughters, and all the poise that many years of responsibility and success had given her. For the first time in those twenty-nine years she could give herself up to enjoyment of the simple social pleasures from which the constant activity of her life had cut her off. She could also find time to record her impressions. The diary which she kept at the time, and which covers the whole year she spent in England, is the only personal record we have of her. From its yellowed pages, covered in cramped, angular writing, there emerges a vigorous, keen and lovable personality. No detail of the trip was too small to record. The young and impetuous girl has come back a mature and kindly woman, wise and balanced, yet showing a rather naive snobbishness in the delight she takes in the tea parties and receptions arranged in her honour. 'Mrs B., a very ladylike woman and one of the most respectable about that part, was very glad to see us.' 'Among our friends was Mrs M. Corte, . . . a very genteel woman.'

Little touches like this show that her position in the colony had not been an easy one for her. Her life had been too full of interesting things, and she was too sensible to let it worry her, but it was 'very gratifying' to be received on terms of perfect social equality by the kind of people who in New South Wales would have considered themselves infinitely beyond her. Among her relatives there was no memory of her childish disgrace: only affection, delight, and a very natural curiosity. 'My arrival became known to all the old inhabitants of Blackburn who had known me in my childhood. The door hardly ever ceased with people coming either out of curiosity or respect.'

Once settled in lodgings in London, she had a great deal of business to attend to. We can imagine the surprise roused in the bosoms of respectable agents when the pleasant-faced, plump little widow from the Antipodes came to conduct her business in person. A miniature painted at this time shows a round face framed by thick, greying hair; large, keen brown eyes behind glasses worn rather low on a small nose; a firm, humorous mouth with upward-curving corners; and a strong chin, whose determined outlines have not yet been obliterated by a tendency to plumpness. There is character and strength in the face, and, judging by the portrait of Jane Penelope, who greatly resembled her, there was once beauty and vivacity.

She is in no way affected by the sense of inferiority that so many 'colonials' experienced on going to London. It is very pleasant to renew old acquaintances, revisit familiar places, but it is not her home. 'I met Mr Jones (a fellow colonist),' she writes soon after her arrival, 'who I believe was as much amaized as I was to see me in London, however we sat down and had a little talk about *our country*.'

There is something very poignant in those words. Four months' journey from the tiny settlement, where she had known life in all its bitterness and its fullness; able, if she so desired, to live very comfortably among the 'respectable' people, who receive her so warmly, she yet turned back to the settlement as her 'country'.

The most pleasurable experience of her trip was renewing acquaintance with relatives, whose warm welcome shows that her original offence was very mild. 'I found my old nurse and her husband, who was both so gratified they hardly knew how contain themselves with joy. The old lady said she was sure she could not have rested in her grave had she not have seen me.' Twenty-nine years of separation had not dimmed Mary's memory of the old woman, and Mary herself showed a childlike delight in being remembered.

It was all so long ago that the sting has gone from her memories, yet on her return to Blackburn, in Lancashire, she was deeply stirred. 'I find it impossible to describe the sensations I felt when coming to the top of Darwin Street – my native home and among my relatives, and on entering my once-grandmother's house where I had been brought up, and to find it nearly the same place as when I left twenty-nine years ago, all the same furniture, most of them standing in the same place, but not one person I knew or who knew me, but was fully requited by my cousin, Miss Alice Hope, who in expectation of our coming, met us at the door with all the affection and love of a sister.'

But it is not all meeting relatives and having tea with 'genteel ladies'. Mrs Reibey intends to go back to the colony, and she is too good a business woman to go back empty-handed. There is always good profit to be made on a good cargo, so she found time to go to 'a manufacturer's wharehouse where I bought a piece of callico measuring 41 yards at a shilling', and 'to Mr Hope's warehouse to look at some cambrik and callico. Gave him an order for a 100 pieces: paid him 8.5.0'.

Her relatives must have found their visitor from the colonies puzzling. She is interested in 'tea-parties', but she has also an insatiable interest in less 'ladylike' pursuits. 'Whent to see the manufactory's of making cotton balls, spining machines,' she writes; and the next week, 'Went to Mr Horrock's Mill and a fine sight it was, but the heat from the steam engine being too oppresive for me – gave me a complete surfeit.'

Every expense incurred on the trip is noted, from 'ten shillings paid on a packet of letters from Mrs Hope' to the doctor's bill, five pounds, three shillings and six, for attendance on 'Eliza and myself for eleven days. Thought it a very exorbitant demand. I was bled with leeches to my temples.'

They went to Glasgow, where, after a round of entertainments and sight-seeing, it was decided to put 'Eliza to school with Miss Duncan in Picardy Place – a most delightful and airy situation. I agreed with her for one year only on a/c of Eliza's bad health but to continue longer if her health proves well, at 52.10 per annum for board and lodging. Tuition in different branches about 24.0.0 more for each young lady.' But all her interests do not dim the thoughts of her family. 'Sept. 13. Dreamed of James last night, the eve of the 13th,' she records with that superstitious anxiety common to mothers everywhere.

'Of birth or blood we do not boast,/Nor gentry does our club afford,/But Ploughmen and the mechanics we/In nature's simple dress record' (Robt. Burns) she writes in her diary, apropos of nothing in particular. Perhaps some memory of the colonial 'gentry' gave particular to Burns's words.

At Edinburgh, in between having their portraits painted, examining a new 'singeing iron', and dancing reels at parties, they went to the Observatory, and saw there the 'Camera Obsqura and the Magnifying glass'. Determined to miss nothing, they 'went to the top of Nelson's Monument and had a view of the Harbour of Leith and the Firth of Forth, and took a basin of hare soup home for which they charged tenpence a basin'. Obviously the Reibey fortune was built up by looking after the pennies.

'There was at that time a great show of wild beasts to be

seen . . .' Mary notes, with all the delight of a small girl at her first circus, but hastens to add in the capacity of a respectable widow, 'I was highly delighted at the sagacity of the elephant.'

In February 1821, she 'took boat to London, pd. three pounds and three shillings,' and on her arrival set about making arrangements for passages to Australia and buying presents for the family. 'Bought today for George 45 vols. of the British Essayists and Gibbon's History of Rome 12 vols.' 'Purchased some Irish Linins. Went to Wakemens the carriers to see about 3 cases with Irish and callico: ordered a double barrelled fowling piece for George. Bought the Encyclopaedia Britanica 20 Vols. 30 guineas.' The difficulties experienced in getting passage to Australia are vividly described in the following pages of the diary. At first arrangements were made to sail in the *Mariner*, but the ship 'could not proceed on her voyage for want of means'. The passengers took complaints to the lord mayor.

'Ever since the 1st of April when he 1st engaged that the ship should sail, I have been living at a very heavy expence and in consequence of my sickness has increased it and God only knows now when we shall get off but I will put my trust in Him who alone can foretell.'

The entries show increasing anxiety. She was constantly ill 'of a violent cough and cold', due apparently to the severity of the northern winter. But she did not waste her time in London. There was Mrs James Reibey's pension to be seen to, and the brief entries rouse a feeling of sympathy in anyone who has had to deal with government departments. 'Went to Mark Lane to enquire about Rebecca's pension.' 13th: 'Called at the Temple to see William Charles Wentworth; staid with him too long till twas too late to go.' 'Staid with him too long!' What did the elderly widow and the young Australian lawyer, burning to return to Australia and join in the struggle for freedom, talk of that day? We would sacrifice many of the 'parties' described in such detail for some slight inkling. Whatever it was, it necessitated a further visit on the 14th, followed by 'another visit to Whitehall to enquire about Mrs James Reibey's pension. Gained all I could after being referred from one to another till I was tired'.

While waiting for the boat to sail she stayed quietly with friends, recovering slowly from her illness. Each Sunday they went to church – in the morning to the Church of England and in the evening to the 'disenting Chapel', and she faithfully reported the text of each sermon. Then, recovering some of her old energy, she went off to the ship and personally supervised 'the disposition of her stores'.

At last the ship was ready to sail, but not before there was 'a great dispute between him (the owner) and the passengers, and on his leaving he was hissed and hooted not without his deserving for a more oppressive villain cannot exist'.

It is pleasant to see that association with gentility has not entirely subdued her, and she gives a further tit-bit that conjures up a delightful picture: 'The owner paid the seamen their advance, the Brokers leaving the ship they was cheered by the passengers and crew, but upon the owner leaving their where nothing but groans and I belive the curses of the major part of both.'

The last entry in the diary throws further light on the trials of passengers setting out on a long voyage. At Portsmouth 'we found the Captain in difficulty in regard to provisions on the ship. Heard that the owner Evans was in gaol; the passengers obliged to consult about paying for their provisions.' But they were really off this time – Eliza had weakened at the last moment and begged to be allowed to return, so Miss Duncan's academy knew her no more. Her reluctance to remain is explained by an announcement in the *Sydney Gazette* soon after their arrival, telling of her marriage to Lieutenant Thomas Thomson.

## V

On her return Mrs Reibey determined to retire from business altogether. She was anxious to dispose of the premises in Macquarie Place and in George Street, but buyers were hard to find. At last John Atkinson bought the George Street property, which did not pass entirely out of the family, for he married Jane Penelope a little later.

Great changes had occurred in the colony during her absence. Sir Thomas Brisbane had succeeded Governor Macquarie, and was entrusted with the duty of introducing a number of unspecified reforms. He was also particularly anxious not to be mixed up with the emancipist quarrel. The simplest way of avoiding it seemed to him to leave the administration of the colony to permanent officials, who were all on the side of the 'Exclusives', and to occupy himself with scientific pursuits in the observatory he had built at Parramatta.

There can be no doubt that his neglect of his official duties enormously strengthened the 'Exclusives', who by now were beginning to be known satirically as the 'Pure Merinos'. All Macquarie's valuable work in regulating private trade was undone. The provision market again fell into the hands of trade monopolists, who not only cornered grain but fixed the prices. Small farmers were in desperate straits; hundreds of farms were seized for debt and numerous land grants fell into the hands of the monopolists.

The reforms eventually introduced were of very great importance. The whole status of the colony was altered; it was no longer a penal settlement, but a free colony, to be entrusted gradually with its own government. There was even a suggestion that transportation should be abolished altogether, but this met with such an outcry from the landowners, who wanted cheap labour, that it was dropped.

Francis Forbes, the first chief justice, tried to introduce trial by jury, against the bitter opposition of the 'Exclusives'. When their objections were over-ridden they doctored the jurors' lists so that not one emancipist appeared on them. William Charles Wentworth (just returned from England) and Wardell began to publish the *Australian*, which enthusiastically advocated freer institutions and bitterly opposed the 'Exclusives'.

So far as Mary Reibey was concerned these were probably the most carefree, if not the happiest days of her life. She and her daughters went off to Tasmania to see the first grandson born in September 1821, and found Thomas the second and Thomas the third prospering. There were the preparations for Eliza's marriage, and, at the ceremony in St James's in December 1821, there were doubtless many envious eyes cast on the fashionable frocks and bonnets brought back from England. There were balls and parties at the house in George Street, and young eligibles – civilian and military alike – flocked to pay court to her charming daughters. At the public ball and supper given in Macquarie's honour on his return from Tasmania, she watched with justifiable pride the lovely Celia moving gracefully through the intricate patterns of the minuet. She was partnered by Thomas Wills, whom she was soon to marry, and her wide brown eyes danced beneath exquisitely arched brows – the only feature she had in common with her mother and Jane Penelope.

Life seemed very rich indeed. But tragedy was very close. In

October 1823, Celia Wills died in her twenty-first year. Over a hundred years later, the wistful loveliness of her pictured face moves one strangely. Even the stilted language of the obituary, in which the *Sydney Gazette* records her death, cannot destroy its pathos. 'In June 1822, she was united to Mr Thos. Wills, to whom she has bequeathed a pledge of the tenderest affection – a sweet little girl. Shortly prior to her confinement about four months since, Mrs Wills caught a violent cold, which fastened on the lungs and originated rapid consumption.'

In November of the same year George died in Tasmania as the result of an accident while hunting. How the thought of that 'fowling piece' must have haunted Mary. He was twenty-three, and, as the *Gazette* wrote, 'He possessed a mind well stored with intellectual attainments. His pursuits were of a literary turn.' But the forty-five volumes of the British essayists and the twelve volumes of Gibbon's *History of Rome* his mother had bought for him must have been practically untouched.

Seeking quiet and retirement, Mrs Reibey moved to a pretty cottage on the bank of the Tank Stream, between Pitt and George Streets.

But, though she retired from active participation in business, she was far too energetic to be idle. In 1825 she was appointed one of the governors of the Free Grammar School, and from then on took a keen interest in its development. No doubt it was from her that George inherited his taste for literary pursuits, for she was one of the subscribers to a volume of Tompson's *Select Poems*, which was brought out in 1825.

Living quietly with her youngest daughter, Elizabeth Anne, in her little cottage on the banks of the Tank Stream, she found that her many business interests kept her busily occupied. In 1827 she bought for a thousand pounds a block of land with a frontage of one hundred and sixty feet to George Street. A few weeks before the marriage of her daugher in May 1829, to Adjutant Joseph Long Innes, of the 39th Dorsetshire Regiment, she made a marriage settlement of a part of the land on the young couple.

Much of her time was spent in church affairs, to which she became increasingly devoted, and at a later date Bishop Broughton speaks of her as 'praiseworthy in the highest degree for her exertions in the cause of religion and of the Church of England, scarcely to be paralleled by anyone I have known'.

While she settled down to a peaceful life, occupied mainly with religious and charitable interests, life in the colony became increasingly turbulent. Darling's administration had antagonized everyone but the 'Exclusives', and the popular party, with the *Australian* as its mouth-piece, was clamouring for the extension of civic rights to emancipists, a greater degree of representation in the Legislative Council, the establishment of a jury system, and freedom of the press. Darling's recall in 1831 was greeted with wild rejoicing, in which Wentworth took a prominent part. Bonfires were lit, the governor burned in effigy, and banners flown bearing the words, 'Down with the Tyrant'.

The exciting events of these days were retailed to Mrs Reibey at first-hand, for her son-in-law, Joseph Long Innes, was appointed a magistrate when he resigned from his regiment, the 39th Dorsetshire, on its departure early in the 1830s. From her cottage in the heart of the town she could take a walk to look at the linen-drapers' shops in Pitt Street, and marvel at the changes that had occurred since she displayed her wares in Entally House half a century before. If she preferred a quieter stroll, she could wander through O'Connell Street, which, with its shrubs and flowers, was considered 'one of the most tasty streets in Sydney'; or, in a different direction, admire the beauties of upper Pitt Street, which, though 'less occupied by expensive buildings, is remarkable for the neatness and cheerful appearance displayed by most of the cottages with which it is lined on either side. The small garden plots here and there, their shaded verandahs, and the regularity of design with many of them display taken together, not only please the eye and gratify the taste, but also have a direct tendency to recall the rustic beauties of old England to the memories of everyone who can think of the land he has left and rejoice in the land now his home.'

Governor Bourke's efforts to improve the conditions of assigned convicts made him very unpopular with the 'Pure Merinos', who already resented his attempts to abolish military juries. At last the emancipist quarrel forced him to resign, and his successor, Gipps, was faced with three great problems – transportation, land laws, and responsible government – all of them aggravated by the bitter enmities among the colonists themselves.

Public opinion in England was strongly in favour of abolishing transportation, but the big land owners in Australia found themselves in a cleft stick. Abolish transportation and there would be no more cheap labour; retain it, and there was no hope of being granted the right to govern themselves.

Even Wentworth, by now actively engaged in squatting, made the decision reluctantly. Mary Reibey, remembering that encounter with the young patriot in the Temple twenty years before, pondered on the curious changes that overtake men and places alike. The popular party won another victory when in 1840 a British Order in Council made Tasmania and Norfolk Island the only convict settlements in Australia. Transportation ceased – during the fifty-three years of the convict system 82,250 convicts had come to Australia.

Life in the city grew too disturbing for Mrs Reibey, and as the location became more congested the little cottage on the Tank Stream was no longer a peaceful refuge. She had a large home built at Newtown, in quiet rural surroundings.

A financial storm in the early 1840s wrecked many of the wealthy families, but she survived it. In 1843 it seemed that the country was on the brink of ruin. The Squatters' Association tried to bring the miserable wage even lower than it was. Most of the private carriages were given up in Sydney, and 'many of these once well-appointed equipages descended in the social scale like their owners, and became common public conveyances'.

Gipps and his council quarrelled bitterly, but, to Mrs Reibey, living peacefully in her country house at Newtown, the stormy happenings in Sydney came only as echoes. She was mainly interested in church work, and content to forget her own troubled past in the happiness of her daughters and their children, though she did sometimes sigh for the good old times, when she saw her grand-daughters going about in those immodest new fashions. It was rather a pity, too, for some of the boys to be so hot-headed about all these political quarrels. She and Thomas had always found it paid better to keep clear of them.

But her peace was shattered by the publication of Cobbold's book on 'Margaret Catchpole' in 1845, which led to wild rumours that the wealthy widow in her dashing 'equipage' was the heroine of Cobbold's story. She was much disturbed, and an unsigned letter of March 1847 states that Dr Nixon, bishop of Tasmania, was entrusted with the task of clearing her on his visit to England. 'A strong belief has arisen, both in Australia and England,' the letter says, 'that the person whose history is related by Mr Cobbold under that designation (and I suppose there can be no doubt that was her real name) is now a rich widow named Reibey at Sydney.

I think you expressed such an opinion yourself, and yet Mr Cobbold ends the "History of Margaret Catchpole" giving the date of her death (1819). Mrs Reibey is exceedingly grieved and annoyed at this opinion, and has commissioned the bishop of Tasmania to use his best endeavours to contradict it officially and upon clear documents. He wishes to be placed in communication with Mr Cobbold.'

That she was still, in spite of her age, interested in business is shown by her purchase in 1847 of Joseph Long Innes's interest in the marriage settlement for three thousand pounds.

The fight for responsible government became more impassioned. Gipps, quite broken down in health, resigned, and with the arrival of Governor FitzRoy, who represented the new creed of colonial freedom, even to the point of independence, it seemed that things would settle down quietly. But the revival of the old system of transportation in a new form set the colony ablaze again.

The Transportation Party, headed by Wentworth, prepared a motion in favour of the perpetuation of transportation, bearing 525 signatures. The Anti-Transportation Association responded with a counter-petition bearing 36,589 signatures, out of a population of 53,000, and passionate threats to 'cut the painter entirely'.

They won. The Order in Council proclaiming Australia a penal colony was revoked, but its revocation only increased the bitter antagonism between the two parties.

With the cessation of transportation, labour conditions gradually improved. The general rush to the goldfields in the following year set wages soaring, and the influx of immigrants, attracted by the fantastic stories of sudden wealth, strengthened the demand for responsible government. This was not achieved without a great deal of conflict between the two political parties. The opposition was led by Henry Parkes, Robert Johnson, Montefiore, Mort, Piddington, and the brilliant and eccentric Daniel H. Deniehy, who remorselessly satirized Wentworth's suggested hereditary nobility as 'this mushroom order of nobility, this bunyip aristocracy', and ironically suggested as the arms of one of 'the full-blooded native aristocrats, a field vert, emblazoned on it the rum-keg of the NSW order of chivalry'.

In 1855 a constitution was granted which placed the destiny of the country in the control of the representatives of the people, whose duty it must be to fight for a 'land where man is bountifully rewarded for his labours and . . . which no more recognizes the supremacy of a class than it does the predominance of a creed' (Deniehy).

On 30 May 1855, Mary Reibey died at her home in Newtown. She was buried beside her husband in the Devonshire Street Cemetery with the simple inscription: 'Mary, widow of the above: Born May 12, 1777. Died May 30, 1855.'

Sixty-three of her seventy-eight years had been spent in the country to which she had come so inauspiciously. She had seen the tiny convict settlement, with its cluster of bark huts, grow to a free city; the rock landing replaced by well-built wharves; the virgin bush recede before the axes of settlers and convicts.

She had known happiness, sorrow and success, and it was the work of such men and women that justified the colony's claim to govern itself, which she lived to see achieved.

Three Australian-born generations survived her, inheritors of the gallant tradition that had enabled individuals to wring full and useful lives out of defeat, and the country itself to forge a nation where none had been before.

# DOROTHEA MACKELLAR

## Release

Out I came on the balcony
To drink the hue of the evening sky,
The nameless colour of summer night –
Blue-green, green-blue as amazonite
But tissued soft as a leaf-hid flower –
Out I came in a magic hour.

Seven black swans flew overhead,
An arrow aimed at the evening star;
Swift, unwavering, so they sped
From the salt lagoons to the west afar,
With a clanging cry as the black bolt flew
By the black Bridge-lattice against the blue.

Sydney's profile was dome and tower,
Beauty spun from the pitying hour:
In lilac, purple and blue and grey
Sydney's waters were whispering 'Stay!'
But there fell the clang of the black swans' cry:
Out and away with them straight flew I.

# ELEANOR DARK

## Caroline Chisholm and her Times

*I*

So much has already been written about Caroline Chisholm that anything in the nature of a mere description of her work and eulogy of her virtues seems superfluous. At this time, however, when the country which she so befriended in its infancy has achieved a century and a half of what has not, perhaps, been altogether progress, it may be not only interesting but salutary for us to remember and acknowledge something of the debt which we owe to her.

But before dealing with that aspect of her life, which particularly affects us as Australians, there are other aspects which deserve notice. Absorbing as the bare record of her almost superhuman endeavours and achievements must always remain, she has a new importance and a new significance when considered in relation to her times.

Caroline Chisholm had three material environments – England, India and Australia – but in all of them the same spiritual environment or *zeitgeist* enveloped her. It is the common habit of mankind – indeed, it is necessary to the preservation of his sanity – to compromise at least here and there with the times in which he lives; but it is only out of his occasional refusals to conform, his determination to alter such aspects of them as anger or revolt him, that changes are made – for better or for worse.

To see Caroline Chisholm clearly, then, one must see her against her background. The exact date of her birth appears to be uncertain, but it took place in the parish of Northamptonshire in England some time during the first decade of the nineteenth century.

The whole of this century was a time of rather disconcerting development. Machines, once begun, developed fast – the first locomotive was built in 1804, the first railway opened in 1825, steamships were beginning to be used. 1835 brought the first electric telegraph and 1851 the first submarine cable. Nothing lagged, but the intelligence and the understanding of man for whose comfort, convenience and betterment these marvels were presumably intended. Man remained much as he had always been – not brutal, but apathetic; not callous, but unimaginative; not unwilling for reforms, but conservative and slow to recognize their necessity.

A. V. Dicey, in his *Law and Public Opinion in England*, has stated that 'there exists at any given time a body of beliefs, convictions, sentiments, accepted principles or firmly rooted prejudices, which, taken together, make up the public opinion of a particular era, or what we may call the reigning or predominant current of opinion . . .'

The quality of the 'predominant opinion' of the nineteenth century may be fairly accurately judged from the following almost incredible extract (from a review of *Jane Eyre*), which was published in the *Quarterly* in 1848:

'Jane Eyre is proud and consequently ungrateful. It has pleased God to make her an orphan, without friends, without money, nevertheless she thanks nobody – least of all her friends, companions and teachers of her lonely youth – for the food and clothing, the care and education they have had the goodness to give her until she could provide for herself. In short, the autobiography of Jane Eyre is an anti-Christian work. It is a long murmur against the well-being of the rich, and the privations of the poor, that is to say, a murmur against the Divine Will . . . It is that tone of discontent which forms the most subtle evil to be combated by the courts, the Christian pulpits, and civilized society.'

And combated it was by all these respectable institutions. It was this attitude, this terrible belief in the perfection and the infallibility of the ruling classes, which reformers of the nineteenth century had to alter, and which, gradually and painfully, they did alter. A procession of dates may give some idea of the slow but steady march of reform. In 1802 the Health and Morals Act laid down, among other things, that the rooms of factories must be washed with quicklime and water twice a year. The prohibition of the slave trade took place in 1806, the partial abolition of the pillory in 1816, and in 1819 the first Factory Act endeavoured to restrain employers from exploiting the poverty of their workers (among whom were children nine years old). In 1820 the whipping of women was abolished and 1822 saw the earliest attempts to forbid cruelty to animals. About 1830 Richard Oastley, infuriated by the horrors of child-labour in factories, published his *Slavery in Yorkshire*, and in 1836 public indignation at the fate of the Tolpuddle martyrs caused a remission of their brutal sentence.

Such events as these, taking place during the childhood and young womanhood of Caroline Chisholm, inevitably suggest that she was not only a person but a portent. Public opinion, recognized as a powerful force in the framing of laws, was being turned during her lifetime, and by a handful of such people as herself, away from the accepted ideas of a society perhaps more smugly and hypocritically complacent in the face of suffering than any society before or since.

Interesting as she is to Australians, therefore, in a narrow and local sense, as part of their brief history of nationhood, she has a wider interest as being part of a movement, one grain of the yeast working. But her significance does not end there, for she was not only a reformer but a female reformer in an age when fearless thinking and independent action were not generally considered desirable, or even quite respectable, attributes of womanhood. Nor was she an isolated woman reformer; so that, again, in another direction she becomes a portent.

In 1792 Mary Wollstonecraft had published her *Vindication of the Rights of Women*, the bell, so to speak, which rang the beginning of a fight which lasted well into the twentieth century, and which, if certain indications in Europe are to be believed, may yet have to be fought again. Caroline Chisholm, though she probably did not know it, was in the forefront of this battle all her life. She was an extraordinarily single-minded woman; a woman who never for one instant lost sight of her objects, which were, quite simply, to alleviate suffering and to further her pet scheme of 'family colonisation'. There is no evidence to suggest that she ever thought of 'women's rights' as a political movement; indeed, one gathers an impression that she might have disapproved of such an idea as being indecorous. Nevertheless, not half a dozen books by Mary Wollstonecraft could have been a more effective 'vindication' than the life of this indomitable woman.

The first public suffrage meeting with a woman in the chair was held as late as 1869, and Winifred Holtby tells us, in her book

*Women*, that it was greeted with hostility and ridicule, public speaking by women being condemned as 'ridiculous and immoral'. But by that time Caroline Chisholm had been speaking in public for years. Her aim was charitable rather than revolutionary (though charity as she saw and practised it was revolutionary enough in those days), and this, perhaps, partially disarmed censure, for, to quote Winifred Holtby again: 'Charity was a respectable, even a fashionable, occupation'. It cannot be too greatly emphasized, however, that the charity which was 'fashionable' and the charity of Caroline Chisholm were two very different things. One was an affair of soup and flannel petticoats, and though these were matters which the practical Mrs Chisholm would never have despised, her own charity was less a mere giving than a giving-up. She gave up her personal comfort, she gave up her leisure, she gave up a great deal of her home life, and the companionship of her children, and she gave up a not inconsiderable amount of their own quite slender resources. She met, of course, the usual censure for this. She should be content to remain in the bosom of her family; she should not leave her home and her children to care for strangers. Charity, in short, should not only begin, but end, at home. The dusting of a room for a necessarily (even in Victorian times) limited family was, and still is, often taken to be a greater, a nobler, a more 'womanly' work than the improvement of the world for an eventually unlimited posterity. Mrs Chisholm most likely did not argue this question even with herself. She saw evils she could redress, she saw suffering she could allay, she saw despair and bitterness which she could dispel, and it is improbable that even during the 'hesitation' of which she tells us she ever really doubted in what direction her duty lay.

The respective attitudes of the average man and the average woman towards the question of human progress might be roughly described as the wide idealistic and the narrow practical. There is no question of comparing their merits or their usefulness; each has its own sphere and function. But it is interesting to notice through the long story of Caroline Chisholm's work that she never deviated an inch from the essentially feminine method and approach. She was far from incapable of seeing a distant and tremendous vision, but a glance was all she spared it from the urgent work which lay beneath her hand. She did not wait to do things in a large and impressive way – she was perfectly content to make a small and a very humble beginning. She looked to the completed structure of a nation, but was content to lay its foundations faithfully, man by man, woman by woman, child by child, seeing in the united family the nucleus, the essential life-cell of progress.

## II

We know little of Caroline's parents beyond the facts that their name was Jones, that they were of a charitable turn of mind, and that Mr Jones, unlike most fathers of the day, not only allowed his children to remain in the room when matters of importance were being discussed, but even, occasionally, asked their opinion. A wounded soldier, sheltered by them during Caroline's early childhood, first told her tales of distant lands, and of the advantages to be gained in them; her father, pausing to listen to her pronounce her childish views, fostered in her a habit of independent thought and confident expression. These details are sparse, but not without significance. When there is added to them the following extract of a letter written many years later by Caroline to a friend in Sydney, it becomes obvious that in the child the vocation of the woman was already awakening:

'My first attempt at colonization was carried out in a wash-hand basin before I was seven years old. I made boats of broad beans; expended all my money in touchwood dolls; removed families . . .' (families, be it noted, not individuals) '. . . located them in the bed quilt, and sent the boats, filled with wheat, back to their friends, of whom I kept a store in a thimble-case.'

Two years after her marriage to Captain Archibald Chisholm she found herself in Madras. Here, almost immediately, she discovered work to do. Eneas Mackenzie, in his *Memoirs of Mrs Caroline Chisholm*, describes the school that she founded there for the daughters and orphans of soldiers, and affords an interesting sidelight upon the times. The room which was first allotted to her for this purpose was, he tells us, near the barracks, but as 'the language and scenes of a barrack room are decidedly unsuitable to the ears and eyes of female youth', she removed the school (and her own household) 'to a district where, from dread of infection, many families of their acquaintance refused to visit them.'

The school, however, one is happy to relate, did not remain

long in this unsalubrious neighbourhood. Its usefulness becoming apparent, it was again removed to a better site, and given the somewhat cumbersome but undoubtedly impressive name of The Female School of Industry for the Daughters of European Soldiers. A few details about this school may be given as illustrations of that practical commonsense that never deserted its founder, and that appears again so vividly during her colonizing schemes. Reading, writing and arithmetic were taught, not only as well as, but hand-in-hand with, housekeeping. The children 'ran' the school themselves. The little girls were formed into a committee to decide upon and arrange the duties to be performed. One set, for instance, had charge of the stores, weighing them out, setting down the prices as they were 'sold' to the girls who, for the time being, were the housekeepers. From an entry in the Housekeepers' Account Book, dated 1 June 1836, and signed by three little girls aged thirteen, twelve and eight, we learn that 'as there was some cold meat left, and a small quantity of rice which would not keep until tomorrow, we made it into pish-pash and gave it to the poor blind woman'. This, no doubt, was approved, for charity to the poor was a regular item in the children's instruction. Wastefulness, however, was not tolerated, and after the entry: 'Extra, two spoonfuls of barley to make barley water for Mary McMillan, who is not very well', we read the ominous query: 'What use did you make of the boiled barley after drawing off the water?'

That question is far from trivial, if one wishes to know and understand Caroline Chisholm. It was not really odd, but quite inevitable, that from such matters as the disposal of two spoonsful of barley she should proceed to the colonization of Australia. Both impulses sprang from a common trait, firmly rooted in her character, and she would not have felt herself less at fault for neglecting the one than the other. Waste, whether of human life, of human labour, or of barley, was abhorrent to her. Years later, in a letter addressed to Earl Grey, upon the relative merits of emigration and transportation, the same note sounds again with an almost passionate earnestness:

'Is it not a lamentable thought, then, my Lord, that deaths should daily result from starvation among British subjects, while in this valuable colony good wheat is rotting on the ground for the want of hands to gather it in; that tens of thousands of fine sheep, droves after droves . . . of fat cattle are annually slaughtered there, and *boiled down* in order to be rendered into tallow for the European market, while the vast refuse is cast into the fields to be devoured by dogs and pigs. Let me, in the name of suffering humanity, entreat of your Lordship to take into . . . consideration this demand for labour, this fearful waste of human food . . .'

The school, as might have been expected, grew in size and influence, but the time came when its founder was forced to leave it in other hands. Captain Chisholm's health being unsatisfactory, it was decided that they should come to Australia, and the government took over and continued the good work which Mrs Chisholm had begun.

The Chisholms sailed for Australia in 1838.

## III

To what kind of country did they come? It may be possible, by the enumeration of a few facts, to give a broad idea of the colony of New South Wales as it was during the few years preceding the arrival of Mrs Chisholm. Its population was 97,912, and the amount of land under cultivation was 92,912 acres. The rate of growth of the colony in this latter respect is indicated by the figures (given by David Collins) in 1791, 780 acres; and by the figures for 1845, 181,556, acres. The estimated expenditure of the government for the previous year had been £32,042/19/10½, and in 1838 Governor Gipps announced to the colonial secretary that '1 Government House, 11 Churches, 4 Gaols, 1 Lunatic Asylum, 1 Watchhouse, 3 Courthouses, 1 National School, 1 Signal House, 1 Police Office, and numerous places of separate confinement' were in the process of being built. All this seems to suggest, if not exactly progress, at least great activity. A local newspaper, the *Colonist*, in an almost lyrical outburst of patriotic self-congratulation, speaks, at the end of 1836, of 'bountiful crops', of the 'luxuriant pasturage' due to 'abundant rains' upon which graze 'our new scarcely numerable flocks and herds'. The flocks themselves are proclaimed to be 'free from disease, plump and healthy, their wool of the finest quality', and there has been an increase in the previous lambing season. In fact, 'the approaching autumn promises to pour into our garners a cornucopia teeming with the mingled bounties of Ceres and Pomona'. In other words, they had had a good season.

Nor is this all: 'Domestic comforts and the elegancies of social life' have made their appearance. 'Aristocratic mansions' are built. Farmers and graziers are 'mounted on high-mettled chargers', or 'roll rapidly along in fashionable barouches, attended by their liveried menials'. And 'in what sense', exclaims the *Colonist*, in a final crescendo of satisfaction, 'can we convey to our friends in the mother-country . . . an adequate idea of SYDNEY?' And it goes on to speak of shops and dwelling houses whose 'dimensions, architectural taste and internal elegance' are 'equal to some of the most respectable private edifices in London', of building ground selling at several thousand pounds an acre, and touches yet again upon 'citizens charioted along in a splendour of equipage . . .'

So far, then, New South Wales in the late 1830s would seem to have been a thriving, prosperous colony, which, in a sense, it was. But across the bright picture of pastoral and industrial development there lie three black shadows – the treatment of convicts, the treatment of emigrants, and the treatment of the Aborigines.

## IV

The American War of Independence ('a thing', as H. G. Wells dryly remarks, 'very shocking to European diplomacy') had, towards the end of the previous century, deprived England of her penal colonies there, to which, since 1619, she had been transporting the overflow of her gaols. But poverty, misery and the recklessness of despair continued to provide in England an unfailing supply of 'criminals' after this avenue for their disposal was blocked, so that the government found itself seriously embarrassed by an accumulation of what one writer of the day termed 'human refuse'. Captain Cook's eulogies of Botany Bay came opportunely, and in 1788 the First Fleet, under Captain Arthur Phillip, cast anchor in Sydney Harbour. But it took many years for England to dispose of those of her sons for whom she had no further use. Newgate, constructed to hold four hundred and eighty prisoners, held, in 1812, nearly eight hundred, and there was similar overcrowding in other gaols. There is no need to stress the conditions that confronted another woman reformer of the period – Elizabeth Fry; it is more necessary to remember that this same England at this time was the home of Jane Austen, and the scene of her delicately ironic, but essentially peaceful, leisurely, and rural novels. Only by some such violent contrast can one imagine the two worlds of nineteenth-century England and understand the sincere and genuine astonishment with which humanitarian efforts were often greeted by quite sane and kindly people.

There was some outcry against the transportation of felons to Australia, just as there had been by such men as Franklin, in the case of America, but no one thought of questioning the transportation of ideas. Governor Phillip might say that he 'would not wish convicts to lay the foundations of an empire'; Caroline Chisholm herself might cry: 'Oh! it is frightful to look upon the monster evil which our penal policy has entailed upon that country!' Walter Savage Landor might lament: '. . . the putrescent weeds/Of Europe, cast by Senates to infect/the only unpolluted continent . . .'

Nevertheless, it seems reasonable to suggest that the main handicap under which the infant colony laboured, the main factor which retarded its growth to nationhood, was not the convict system, but the fact that the real preoccupation of the 'mother-country' was, not to develop, but to exploit. It was the official attitude, and, all too often, it was the individual attitude, persisting through the century, stimulated during its latter half by the discovery of gold. The following extract from a letter, written in 1852 by a young man to his father, illustrates this viewpoint:

'We have now made up our minds to stick tooth and nail to business for the next three years, and then, hurrah for home! with sufficient, I trust, to keep us there without ever again visiting the colonies.'

This, of course, was a perfectly natural viewpoint. The fact remains that such people contributed nothing to the development of the country; their aim was to take out, not to put in. The convicts, on the other hand, and later on the free settlers who had been driven by pauperism to try their luck in a new land, had every incentive to develop the country. From now on it was their country. If there should still remain in the minds (or perhaps one should say the emotions) of conventional people a feeling of shame for a country thus populated, the most cursory study of the records would remove it. Passing over the question of whether one might not reasonably feel less abashed by descent from even the worst of the convicts than from some of those responsible for such a system, the excellent Caroline Chisholm and others have left testimony that cannot be ignored. It would be ridiculous and untrue to say or imply that the majority of the convicts were not, upon their arrival, idle, ignorant anti-social people. Governor Phillip and that careful chronicler, David Collins, both speak of their malingering, their quarrelling, their riotousness, their pilfering from the stores. But what is more interesting and more important to us is the reliable testimony of Mrs Chisholm as to what happened to them when, as emancipists, they found themselves free in a country where their decent instincts had a chance to develop. In the same letter to Earl Grey which has already been quoted she begs to be allowed to give her 'humble testimony to the sterling worth and exemplary conduct, as a body, of the emancipists of New South Wales. At a time when slander outruns truth and charity as regards the moral character of that people, I must honestly tell your Lordship that as parents their extreme, nay, I must call it nervous anxiety, regarding the moral and religious welfare of their children; the efforts they make to educate them; the miles they travel to attend a place of worship on the Sabbath; their deep sympathy for the unfortunate; their Christian liberality and charity; their open-hearted hospitality, have endeared numbers of them to my remembrance'.

And again: 'Often, my Lord, have I heard the emancipist at family prayers return thanks to Almighty God that his children were not in a country where they might be tempted by hunger to perpetrate a crime.'

These were the lucky ones. Others, after a few years of the 'discipline' meted out to them, not only found but welcomed death. The misery and degradation of their own lives were such that inevitably life itself lost value and sacredness. It became their practice to draw lots, the one upon whom the lot fell murdering someone, in cold blood and without animosity, simply to secure for himself the release of death, and for his fellows the respite of a journey to Sydney, where they were taken as witnesses to the murder.


## V

So much for the convicts. Such horrors need not be stressed, but must not be forgotten or excluded from any fair picture of the times. But passing on to the question of the Aborigines, it is interesting to remember that in Governor Phillip's day a group of these 'untutored savages', who, until quite recently, were spoken of and written of in tones of indulgent contempt, to whom even the benign Judge Therry refers as 'this poor, inferior race', expressed horror and repugnance at the sight of a flogging which the governor, with excellent, if mistaken, intentions, had summoned them to witness. The Aborigines had their own ideas. The malefactor in their tribe was killed with spears by the rest, but he was given his shield and allowed to defend himself while he could. His life was taken from him, but his human dignity never, and to see white men so degrade and humiliate their fellows was a lesson in 'civilization' which the blacks must have long remembered.

For many years there went on, sporadically, a kind of guerilla warfare between blacks and whites. The attitude of many, though not a majority, of the squatters and settlers was voiced by the murderers who were tried and condemned to death for the atrocious Myall Creek massacre in 1838, in which not less than twenty-eight entirely inoffensive blacks, mostly women and children, were deliberately butchered with rifles and swords. The murderers were not only aghast, but honestly incredulous when they were convicted. They protested that they did not know they had done anything wrong, as it had *been so frequently done in the Colony before.*' Governor Gipps, in a letter to the colonial secretary, says of the murderers: 'They all stated that they thought it extremely hard that white men should be put to death for killing blacks.'

It must be stressed, in fairness to the authorities, that no kind of official sanction was ever given to persecution of the blacks. Indeed, the instructions given to Governor Phillip and all his successors were to spare their lives and to endeavour to 'civilize and convert' them. The honesty of these intentions cannot be doubted; their commonsense is another question. A nomad race finds its country invaded, its streams polluted, its hunting grounds commandeered, cleared, fenced, sown with crops. Its food supply is affected. The white men hunt and kill the kangaroos as a matter of course, but if the hungry blacks kill a sheep for a meal there is the devil to pay.

That the blacks should occasionally have attacked the whites is understandable, excusable, inevitable. That the whites should have defended themselves when attacked is also understandable. Massacre and poisoning are different matters; these, with disease, alcohol and 'civilization', have come near to exterminating a race to which, too late, we are beginning to give the respect which it deserved.

## VI

The emigrants seem to have been handled with as little imagination as were the convicts and the blacks. At the time of the Chisholms' arrival, emigration under the bounty system was just coming into vogue. Under this system the government paid a 'bounty' of thirty pounds for a married man and his wife, five pounds for a child, fifteen pounds for an unmarried female between fifteen and thirty, and ten pounds for an unmarried male mechanic or farm servant. On arrival in the colony, they were required to exhibit testimonials of good character to a board appointed for the purpose. A contemporary writer says of this system: 'On the whole, it was very successful,' and goes on to remark, 'It partially failed, however, on account of the unseaworthiness of the vessels, the great mortality amongst emigrants, occasioned by the bad ships and bad diet, and the immorality . . . that prevailed on board. It further partially failed from the frauds practised on the government by the introduction of ineligible persons.' It is a little difficult to see from whose point of view it can have been considered 'on the whole very successful'; but with unseaworthy ships, bad diet, immorality and many deaths it seems evident that it cannot have been from the emigrants'. The evils of such a system, the boundless opportunities it afforded for brutality, exploitation and 'graft', must indeed have been obvious enough. Bounty agents scoured the United Kingdom urging the poor to emigrate, regardless of their suitability, painting in glowing colours the life that awaited them in their new land, ignoring or evading the requisite 'certain standard' in their haste to fill their ships and reap their 'bounty'. How the emigrants were fed, housed and treated on the long four months' voyage, what became of them when they landed, friendless and often penniless, in a strange country, seems to have concerned the government not at all.

They remained, therefore, in the city. No one, apparently, took the smallest interest in their plight. They had no homes and often no money. The total wealth of a party of sixty-four girls who landed about this time amounted to fourteen shillings and a penny halfpenny. There were, in 1841, six hundred respectable women unemployed in Sydney. Young girls of good character roamed the streets by day and slept under rocks in the Domain at night.

This, then, was the colony to which Caroline Chisholm came – in the nick of time. Aristocratic mansions, homeless emigrants, liveried menials, despairing convicts, squatters on high-mettled chargers, shops, houses, gaols, lunatic asylums and churches. It was called, constantly, 'a new land', but it was only a new occupation of a very ancient land, a tide of human life, surging recklessly over a land it spared no time to know, or to attempt to know.

## VII

It is small wonder that, with such conditions existing in Sydney, Caroline Chisholm did not remain long in seclusion at Windsor, where, upon their arrival, the Chisholms had made their home. Nevertheless, she did not begin her crusade without some inward doubts and tremors. Her own words can tell better than any others of the battle she fought with herself before embarking upon the work which was to claim the rest of her life:

'For three weeks I hesitated and suffered much . . . as a female and almost a stranger in the country I naturally felt diffident . . . my delay pressed on my mind as *a sin*, and when I heard of a poor girl suffering distress and losing her reputation in consequence I felt that I was not *clear of her sin* for I did not do all I *could* to prevent it . . . On the Easter Sunday I was enabled at the altar of Our Lord to make an offering of my talents to the God who gave them. I promised to know neither *country nor creed* but to serve all impartially . . . I felt my offering was accepted and that God's blessing was on my work; but it was His Will to permit many serious *difficulties* to be thrown in my way and to conduct me through a rugged path of deep humiliation.'

Her difficulties were indeed serious and might have discouraged her. She sought and, after some delay, obtained an interview with the governor, Sir George Gipps. Sir George does not seem to come out of the matter very well. Samuel Sidney says of him: 'Like a true despot, every political opponent was, in his eyes, a rebel. He was a vain man, too, and could not endure that any measure likely to be creditable to its author or of benefit to the colony

should originate with other than himself.' His despatches,
however, seem to suggest a conscientious and fair-minded man,
and the vigour and humanity with which he championed the
Aborigines must always be remembered to his credit.

At all events, his support of Mrs Chisholm in her enterprise
was less than lukewarm. One seems to hear, too, the 'vain man'
in his own description of their first interview:

'I expected to have seen an old lady in white cap and spectacles
who would have talked to me about my soul. I was amazed when
my *aide* introduced a handsome, stately young woman, who
appeared to argue the question as if she thought her reason, and
experience, too, worth as much as mine.'

Time has already shown them to have been worth a good deal
more. But Sir George needed, it appears, 'much persuasion'. The
author of *The Emigrants' Guide to the Australian Gold Fields* tells
the story with a good deal of indignation. Having at last consented
to allow her the use of a low wooden shed in which to shelter
her homeless girls, Sir George made the 'remarkable condition'
that the government must be guaranteed against all possible
expense.

'As you read the narrative furnished by Mrs Chisholm's own
pen of the annoyance . . . to which she was subjected in this
wretched, filthy place, you must blush, reader, for the
Government of England, that hands over the interests of wealthy
colonies, peopled by many thousands of your fellow-countrymen
and women to the protection and control of such men as Sir
George. While, as she tells us, hundreds of single women of good
character were roaming the streets of Sydney . . . this man, the
very head of the colonial administration, the representative and
deputy of the Queen of England, stipulates with a benevolent
woman . . . that the Government – whose officers, be it
understood, conveyed these poor creatures to Sydney – shall not
be put to a few pounds' expense.'

Lady Gipps, however, 'seems to have rendered some assistance,
or to have shown some indications of sympathy', and Mrs
Chisholm says of her, gratefully, 'She strewed a few flowers in
my path.' It is only fair to say, also, that Sir George himself,
though not until much later, when the value of Mrs Chisholm's
work could no longer be denied, made handsome amends:

'I cannot give a stronger ev:dence of the economy of the people
working for themselves than by referring to what has been done

by Mrs Chisholm, and I am glad of this opportunity of doing justice to that lady's exertions, and do it with much greater pleasure and satisfaction from having, at the commencement of her labours, thrown cold water on her plans.'

The governor's was not by any means the only opposition which Mrs Chisholm encountered. Samuel Sidney says: 'The most imperious section of the employer class saw no advantage from the protection of the unemployed. The officials saw more work, some supervision, and no increase of pay.' Nor were these the only obstructionists. The question arose (and this would be comic if it were not tragic) of religion. One might not, surely, be considered over-optimistic in assuming that, whatever their differences upon other points, all religions might find themselves at one upon the very simple question of sheltering homeless girls. Mrs Chisholm herself was a Roman Catholic, but it will be remembered that 'at the altar of our Lord' she had promised to know neither creed nor country. Many Protestants seemed unable to believe in this impartial charity. She met, on all sides, suspicion and scepticism – oddly enough, not only from Protestants because they feared she would proselytise, but also from Roman Catholics, because they feared she would not! One member of this church referred to her as 'a lady labouring under amiable delusions'.

Not only publicly, and from avowed antagonists, but privately, from so-called friends, came opposition. She relates herself how at this time she 'received a letter from one, of so painful a nature that I am astonished how my mind held out . . . I found I should be driven from the field by those who ought to raise the standard and cry, "On! On!" I did not think it possible another blow could be hurled against me, but a number of the *Chronicle* was sent to me and my attention was directed to a letter; from the hand of a friend came a missile of great strength – I felt it keenly; no other person in the colony could have thrown more serious difficulties in my path; these things are *permitted* to try our faith . . .'

Other trials were also permitted, but Mrs Chisholm, undaunted if not quite undismayed, went quietly ahead with her plans. The first and most glaring need was a shelter of some kind for homeless and friendless girls, and the wooden shed so grudgingly bestowed by the governor now became their refuge. Judge Therry describes it as 'built of slabs through which the wind made free entrance by day and night', and it is impossible to do better than turn to

Mrs Chisholm's own description of the first night she spent in it, for it affords us, not only a picture of the place, but another sidelight upon the indomitable character of the woman herself:

'On closing the door I reflected on what I had been compelled to endure for forty-nine square feet. My first feelings were those of indignation that such a trifle had been so long withheld; but better feelings followed . . . I soon observed to do any good I must sleep on the premises, and as soon as Mr Merewether was aware of my determination he gave me the best room then vacant. I cannot say vacant, for it was used as a storeroom. This was, however, cleared for my accommodation and, having been busy all day, I retired, weary, to rest. My courage was put to the proof at starting. Scarce was the light out than I fancied from a noise I heard that dogs must be in the room, and, in some terror, I got a light. What I experienced on seeing rats in all directions I cannot describe; my first act was to throw on a cloak and get at the door . . . my second thoughts were, if I did so, my desertion would cause much amusement and ruin my plan. I therefore, lighted a second candle and seated myself on my bed . . . until three rats, descending from the roof, alighted on my shoulders. I felt that I was getting in a fever and that, in fact, I should be very ill before morning – but to be outgeneralled by rats was too bad . . . I had two loaves and some butter (for my office, bedroom and pantry were one); I cut them into slices, placed the whole in the middle of the room, put a dish of water convenient, and with a light by my side I kept my seat on the bed, reading *Abercrombie* and watching the rats until four in the morning. I at one time counted thirteen, and never less than seven did I observe at the dish during the entire night.'

But still another trial was in store for her – the hardest of all. The family life of Caroline Chisholm is difficult to reconstruct, her biographers having been mainly concerned with her public activities. We know that, in all her undertakings, she received the loyal support and co-operation of her husband and, later, of her elder children, but we are given no picture of her as a wife and mother with her family. We know that she had six children; many modern women would regard this alone as constituting a life-work. We are told nothing (Victorian delicacy, perhaps, forbade it?) of when they were born and of how Mrs Chisholm contrived, in the midst of her incessant and often very strenuous work, to bear and rear them. But one thing we may confidently assume – that the woman who founded the school for little girls in Madras, the women who later spared herself no fatigue and no humiliation in re-uniting workhouse children in England with their parents in Australia was a good and devoted mother. We know, at all events, that she had at least three children at the time when she began her work in Australia and the necessity for leaving her family when she found that she must sleep at the 'home' must have been a great grief to her. To alleviate this very natural loneliness she tells us that she left one child at Windsor and kept two with her in Sydney. Presently she found it advisable to send the elder of these two back to Windsor, but she still could not find it in her heart to part with the third – 'my youngest'. By this time the 'home' was crowded, and people were also sleeping in tents, and when some sickness broke out among the children another battle with herself had to be fought to its bitter end. She tells how, one evening, she found a woman waiting for her to beg a white gown 'to make her dead bairn decent'. That was the end of the struggle. She says: 'I went into my room, packed up my little fellow's wardrobe and the next day he was at Windsor. This was the last sacrifice it was God's will to demand.'

From this time her work progressed steadily. Her immediate aim was to shelter the homeless, but it was obvious that this, to be practical, must be followed up by finding them suitable employment. She, therefore, established a kind of registry office and drew up a form of agreement in triplicate, one copy of which was to be given to the employee, another to the employer, and the third filed for the office. Judge Therry says of these documents: 'The validity of even one of these contracts has never been questioned in the proceedings before magistrates under the Master and Servants' Act.' She sent out questionnaires to various country districts, seeking to find what openings there were for employment, and she formed committees in the country centres to aid her in this work. When it is remembered how slow, in those days, were the means of communication, this alone must have been a formidable task.

She appealed to the public for subscriptions and, after a time, with the aid of the press (to which she refers with gratitude and appreciation), these began to come in, so that in a report issued a few months after the opening of her 'home' she was able to write:

'Since the establishment of the institution 735 young women have been provided with situations; of this number 291 have been distributed among country districts. Pecuniary assistance has been afforded to 42 persons and 263 have received donations of provisions. The amount of subscriptions received was £156, the expenditure £154, cash in hand £2; debts, none.'

In the matter of providing employment in the country for her girls, she found herself confronted by a new difficulty. Fresh from the United Kingdom, ignorant and credulous, many of them never having set foot beyond some crowded city, these girls had been terrified by stories of blacks and bushrangers. Thus Mrs Chisholm's first effort in this direction was frustrated by the girls themselves, who, when the dray arrived, which had been hired to take them to their destination, flatly refused to go. Mrs Chisholm kept her own counsel, not wishing this anticlimax to become public property, but she did some quiet thinking and decided that if they would not go alone she herself must take them.

Thus began those epic journeys with later inspired a versifier in London *Punch* to write:

> Who led their expeditions? And under whose command
> Through dangers and through hardships sought they
>     the promised land?
> A second Moses, surely it was who did it all,
> It was a second Moses, in bonnet and in shawl.

It was not long before she found that she must advise and provide for not only the emigrant girls, but their menfolk, too. 'Her journeys became longer and her parties larger. 147 souls left Sydney in one party, increasing on the road to 240, Mrs Chisholm leading the way on horseback.'

Innumerable stories are told of these strange pilgrimages, and their leader became in time a kind of legend to the country folk whom, during this period of her work, she learned to know so well and to respect so highly. A rather touching story is told of a couple of emancipists who, pathetically anxious that their children should have the advantages of learning, which they had never had themselves, had bought some books which they proudly showed to Mrs Chisholm upon one of her visits. Knowing them unable to read, Mrs Chisholm voiced her doubts as to the suitability of these books for young minds, and hardly were the words out of her mouth before the books were on the fire. No thought of their cost, or of the self-denials which their purchase had involved, and no consideration whether it might not be possible to re-sell them could have stopped this impulsive action. Mrs Chisholm had said they were not good books; into the fire with them!

One point of considerable interest stands out in the whole of Caroline Chisholm's career. She was essentially a practical woman, but she never allowed herself to be bullied by money. She performed a major work of national importance, and though, in the end, money was forthcoming from public subscription and private donations, she embarked upon it quite calmly, almost without funds. Here her faith must have supported her. One imagines her serenely reassuring herself and others with: 'God will provide.' Conceptions of the Deity may vary, but the old text, 'God Is Love,' can offend nobody, and if that definition is accepted God did indeed provide. He provided through the hearts of the country people; settlers, emancipists and station-owners alike gave her and her bands free lodging, conveyance and food. She tells: 'Mr William Bardley, a native of this colony, authorized me to draw upon him for money, provisions, horses or anything that I might require, but the people met my efforts so readily that I had no need to draw upon him for a sixpence. At public inns the females were sheltered, and I was provisioned myself without charge: my personal expenses during my seven years' service amounted to only £1/18/6.'

Even Campbelltown, Parramatta and Liverpool, to which at different times she escorted parties, must have been, in those days of bad roads and horsedrawn transport, quite sufficiently trying journeys; but when one imagines her setting out for Maitland, Yass, Gundagai, Goulburn and Bathurst one is amazed at her sheer physical endurance. When one remembers that only about twenty years earlier the first white woman had crossed the mountains to Bathurst, a journey that occupied eighteen days, one finds it almost incredible that she performed such journeys, not once or twice, but many times.

Judge Therry, in his *Reminiscences*, gives the following picture:

'I remember as though it were yesterday meeting her on the Goulburn road, as early as five o'clock in the morning, when the first burst of an Australian spring loads the air with the perfume of acacias, and the glades of the open forest are clothed in a mantle of bright green . . . Mrs Chisholm herself, wrapped in a loose cloak, was seated on the top of a dray, laden with casks and bales of goods – provisions for a settler at Goulburn. Beside her and around her were seated twelve or fourteen young girls. Alongside the dray walked about thirty others. They travelled on "the ride and walk plan", the walking girls taking their seats on the dray in turn after a walk of four or five miles . . . These girls Mrs Chisholm was taking to distribute in the interior, where she had previously procured employment for them in farms whose good repute she had carefully ascertained.'

Domestic situations were not the only ones which she found for her charges. Women were scarce, wives were wanted, and none had a higher opinion of family life than Mrs Chisholm. 'I should not,' she said once, 'feel the interest I do in female emigration if I did not look beyond providing families with female servants – if I did not know how much they are wanted as wives, and how much moral good they may spread forth in society as wives.' Her methods in this direction were the essence of tact and decorum. She pursued the simple and sensible plan of finding out where wives were needed, ascertaining the good moral character and 'honourable intentions' of the available bachelors, and then finding domestic situations for suitable girls somewhere in the neighbourhood, and always under the wing of a reputable matron. Thus the strictest conventions were observed, and nature was left to bring this innocent match-making to a happy conclusion.

It was indeed Caroline Chisholm's most passionate belief that the violent disruption of families was one of the worst aspects of the existing system. Many of the emigrants had been forced to leave their wives behind them. Many married couples had been forced to part with one or more of their children, who remained in workhouses in England against the longed-for time when their parents could send for them. To all such people Caroline Chisholm proved herself a sympathetic and a practical friend. The instinct which had led the little girl to move families of dolls across the stormy waters of the wash-basin survived strongly in the woman, and, as usual, she not only sympathised but acted. She determined to return to England, there to put before the authorities the truth about these people and their needs.

But it was not only, as she realized very clearly, the authorities who had to be convinced. Emigration, owing to the abuses already described, was in bad odour among the poor of England, and it can hardly be wondered that they hesitated over what must have seemed likely to be a leap from the frying pan into the fire.

To gain their confidence, to put before them, without embellishing its advantages or minimizing its hardships, a true account of the country to which they would be giving their future was obviously her first, if not her hardest, task. She knew that wordy official documents and high-flown official promises would meet with nothing but a well-merited scepticism, and she sought with her customary wisdom to give them the one thing they could, and would, trust – the testimony of their own friends and relatives.

During her long pilgrimages into the country she never missed an opportunity of talking with the humble people she encountered, but to talk was not enough. She explained to them her aims and plans. Instantly trusting her, they were eager to help. 'In the ploughed field,' as she says, 'with the plough for my table,' stories were taken down, verbatim, from their own lips, of their experiences in the colony. No attempt was made to alter their rude phrasing – these were to be their own voices speaking to their own people at home. More, from each person who commissioned her to seek out a friend or a relative she demanded some trifling token, or some story, or some joke, or some memory known only to themselves. These were her guarantees. The statements which, when collected, she called *Voluntary Information from the People of New South Wales*, make poignant reading. Statement no. 18, for instance, is a letter from Peter R——, dated September 1846, to his brother in Ireland:

'My dear Brother i am sorry to hear the distressing news that i hear from Ireland of starvation – sickness – i thank my God for leaving it the time i did . . . This is a fine, plentiful country – there is no person starving here – i am sure that the dogs in Sydney destroys more beef and bread than all the poor in ireland can afford to eat . . .'

There is a touching and ingenious humour about some of the entries. This one, no. 16, from T. F., Galway, 4 August 1845, seems to indicate that already the Australian national diet was superseding that of Ireland:

'We live pretty well here. Now put it down in three rows – it will look better when it's printed; we have:

| For breakfast | – bread | meat | tea |
| For dinner | – bread | meat | tea |
| For supper | – bread | meat | tea |

with milk, butter and eggs; in truth we live well. We grows

potatoes, but don't eat so many as we did at home.'

Ellen W——, of London, in statement no. 5, 11 March 1846, says:

'I arrived in 1833; I am married to George W——. I wish to have out my sister . . . now mind you tell her that her sister, Mary Ann, is married well and lives in the Goulburn district. My brother is doing well. Neither of us have ever wanted for anything in this country . . . We pay eight shillings a week rent, but it is well we get on. Oh, what a difference there is between this country and home for poor folks. I know I would not go back again – I know what England is. Old England is a fine place for the rich, but the Lord help the poor.'

Mrs Chisholm said once: 'The information I give may be depended upon. I will state nothing but facts.' In that rigid adherence to truth lay her influence with the poorer people; they knew that what she told them was, to use a colloquialism which their descendants have coined, 'dinkum'. But she knew to her cost that mere truth, unsupported by documentary evidence, had little weight with officialdom, and it was with officialdom that she must do battle when she returned to London. Taking with her her statements, and a mass of names, dates and addresses, she and her family sailed for England, which they reached in 1846.

But her seven years of labour had, by now, won some recognition. Scepticism was no longer possible in the face of actual achievement. During her stay in Australia she had provided, in one way or another, for eleven thousand souls, and her departure was the scene of a great public demonstration. Crowds assembled, speeches were made, a testimonial and a piece of plate were presented. At least one poem (more remarkable for its enthusiasm than for its literary merit) was inspired. It concluded:

> Say ye who hold the balance of the sword,
> Into your lap the wealth of nations poured,
> What have ye done with all your hireling brood
> Compared with her, the generous and the good?
> Much ye receive and little ye dispense,
> Your aims are paltry and your debts immense,
> Your toil's reluctant – freely hers is given –
> You toil for earth, she labours still for Heaven.

## VIII

Arriving in England, she set about her plans without delay. She had three main objects which she kept steadily in view – the re-uniting of families, the arrangement of a safe and easy method by which successful emigrants in New South Wales might send small sums of money to relatives in England, and the improving of conditions upon emigrant ships.

The first involved colossal labours. Armed with her *Voluntary Information* and her tokens of good faith, she sought out, either personally or by letter, the friends and relatives of the settlers and emancipists to whom she had promised her aid. Her weekly postage bill was one pound. From Ireland alone she received five thousand letters. The sad plight of children separated from their parents received her particular attention, and she began by arranging methodically, dated and docketed, the particulars she had collected relating to each case. She must soon have become a thorn in the flesh of Her Majesty's land and emigration commissioners, to whose offices in Park Street she went grimly, day after day, through a whole winter, 'when the snow often lay ankle-deep in the streets', to plead the cause of the parents whose boundless faith in her she was determined to deserve.

She encountered delay, evasion, discouragement. But having at last gained an interview, and having been met with polite scepticism, she produced what she knew must impress them – documentary evidence. It was said of her in Australia that she never made a claim or a charge which she was not fully prepared to prove, but the commissioners in England did not know her – yet. She liked facts. She liked evidence. She liked to have things down in black and white. At the first breath of doubt, neat packets of paper were produced; one can almost pity officialdom, perspiring gently as the relentless array of names, dates and descriptions left no loophole for further evasion. 'John Smith, aged so-much, and Eliza, his wife, sailed from Liverpool on such-and-such a date in the ship so and so, leaving behind them two of their children, James and Henry, aged five and six years respectively . . .'

After a few such recitals, they surrendered. 'That will do, Mrs Chisholm. We are quite satisfied.' And two shiploads of children were transferred from English workhouses to Australian farms.

The second matter, that of arranging for the transference of money, was also adjusted. The cost of transmitting ten pounds had hitherto been the same as the cost of transmitting one hundred pounds, so that many of the settlers who were anxious to send small sums home in order to hasten the arrival of their families in Australia were unable to do so. Mrs Chisholm, however, after an interview with the managers of a leading London bank, persuaded them to undertake the receipt by their colonial agents of small remittances. Thus another part of her mission was fulfilled.

As might have been expected, she met with even greater opposition to her third reform. The shipowners had hitherto made a handsome profit from overcrowding their ships, and if a few of their passengers happened to die on the voyage it meant rations saved and a still larger profit. They therefore denounced Mrs Chisholm, protesting that if such improvements as she advocated were made upon their ships it would rob them of ten per cent, and did not hesitate to suggest that her philanthropic schemes were merely a cloak for her own mercenary aims.

But Mrs Chisholm, by now, was not playing an entirely lone hand. She had been working indefatigably upon the development of a scheme which she had long cherished and which eventually became the Family Colonization Loan Society. She had no faith at all in government controlled emigration and spoke her mind vigorously:

'I say that neither the government nor the parishes can give us a sound and satisfactory system of colonization; they may give us convict emigration, exile emigration, pauper emigration, but what they cannot give us is a wholesome system of national colonization. Nothing but what is voluntary is deserving of the name national.'

In 1850, having carefully prepared full details of the working of the society that she proposed to form, and having obtained the names of a number of respectable people who had already paid instalments towards a passage to Australia, she enlisted the help of many eminent people, including the Earl of Shaftesbury (then Lord Ashley), and a sum of money was raised to launch the scheme.

Mrs Chisholm felt very strongly that loans, and not gifts, were desirable. Intending emigrants were required to become members of the society. Certificates of good character had to be produced, and these, sent ahead to the colony, and bearing the society's seal, were of great use to the emigrants upon their arrival. These people were also expected to demonstrate, by persistent thrift and industry, their real desire to try their fortunes in a new environment and their qualities for succeeding in it when they arrived. When they had saved a certain amount of their passage money, the society advanced them the rest, which they were expected to repay by instalments from their earnings in Australia. In order to economize the funds of the society, Captain Chisholm agreed to return to Australia and act as the society's agent there. Mrs Chisholm continued to advocate most earnestly the desirability of whole families emigrating together; she saw in the tragedies of parting, which she had watched so often, not only the grief of the participants, but a potential danger to society.

Not all the emigrants, however, had families and Mrs Chisholm realized very clearly the importance of the state of mind of such people upon their departure. Friendless, they joined a ship upon which, in acute discomfort, and often under relentless persecution, they were to live with total strangers. Young women travelling alone were unprotected, theft was common, they knew little or nothing of the land to which they were going. Mrs Chisholm, as usual, chose the simple, the intimate, the rational remedy.

She found a room near her own home and began her famous 'group meetings'. She had no need to seek out intending emigrants now – they flocked to her. She was so well known that a letter from an emigrant girl in Australia, addressed to her as *'Mrs Chisholm, the Emigrants' Friend, England or elsewhere'*, reached her without delay.

At these meetings Mrs Chisholm spent hours answering questions and describing conditions in Australia. Sometimes she found some settler home on a visit and persuaded him to come and tell of his experiences. No detail was too small for her attention. One of her talks began: 'The best kind of shoe to wear on board ship has moderately stout soles and no heels.' In one corner of the room she caused to be erected an exact model, in size and fitting, of a berth on one of the ships. Again, she found herself with homeless girls on her hands, and again she made provision for them in lodgings near her home. Her average day's work has been described by Eneas Mackenzie. It began about 9 am, when the door of her house was besieged by intending emigrants, with whom she dealt in turn. Her daily mail consisted of about one hundred and forty letters. This attended to, she would set out for the docks and go on board the ships to assure herself that conditions would measure up to her standard. Carpenters and ship-fitters received her instructions; provisions were inspected. Then she would return to the city to transact bank and other business. In the evening anything from forty to sixty people would desire and obtain interviews with her. And her last action for the day was to go to the girls' lodging, enquire into their day's activities and assure herself that all were safely settled for the night.

Between September 1850 and July 1852, the society despatched seven ships to Australia, containing 1,288 adults, 475 children and 68 infants. Public meetings were held at their departure, Mrs Chisholm explaining the principles of self-supporting emigration to vast crowds of interested people, and the voyagers set out under very different conditions from those in which earlier emigrants had left their native land. Mrs Chisholm had insisted upon structural alterations to the ships so that reasonable comfort and privacy was now possible. She had insisted upon pure drinking water and an ample supply for washing. She had prepared exhaustive lists of all that it was necessary or desirable for the emigrants to take with them. But, what was far more important, she had insisted upon – and attained – an attitude of hope and confidence. In 'the back street at Islington', talking to the people who came to her for information and advice, she had appealed for the co-operation which, in her experience, the poor at least had never failed to give. That they did not fail now is shown from the following account by Eneas Mackenzie of the departure of the society's first ship, the *Slains Castle*:

'On Monday Mrs Chisholm went on board to bid the emigrants farewell. The men all came on deck and seated themselves around their noble patron and friend. . . . They unanimously pledged themselves as Christian fathers and heads of families to exercise a parental control and guardianship over all orphans and friendless females proceeding with the family groups, to protect them as their children; and to allow them to share the same cabins as their daughters.'

When the time came for her to take her leave of the women 'many wept aloud'. A young Jew clasped her in her arms, calling her 'my dear mother'. Old women prayed for 'the blessing of God to be her portion', and the last cheer given was 'for Mrs Chisholm's children'.

But now there came news from Australia which made it unnecessary for Mrs Chisholm and her society to 'stimulate' emigration any further. The discovery of gold changed the whole face of the situation, so that Mrs Chisholm, her work in England done, was able to rejoin her husband in Australia in 1854. Before this, however, the private shipowners had to a great extent followed the lead of the society in providing adequate accommodation in their vessels, and the horrors of emigrant ships belonged to the past.

By now Caroline Chisholm was something of a personage. *The Illustrated London News* offered her this tribute upon her departure:

'Caroline Chisholm has concluded seven years of hard, of unthankful, of successful work in England, and sailed to renew her labour of love in Australia where, fourteen years ago, she began what has ever since been the business of her life. Fourteen years ago, on the wharves of Sydney Harbour, she saw and pitied the droves of ignorant, outcast, wretched emigrants who . . . were cast out at the close of the voyage to shift for themselves, without a friend or a shelter, to starve, to labour or to steal. No matter; no one cared. How she collected these destitute wretches, how she encouraged them even to honest work . . . and protected the women, and led whole armies from the miseries of Australian towns to the plenty of the far interior . . . is now well known and justly appreciated. Seven years of active practical colonization in Australia have been succeeded by seven not less active years in England, where the government has been taught its duty, the shipowners their true interest, and the labouring classes the lesson of self-dependence and co-operation.'

Australia also now had eulogies to offer her. The Committee of the Legislative Council of New South Wales, in a report, 'desire to record their grateful sense of the valuable services of a lady, to whose benevolent exertions on behalf of the unemployed, as well as free emigrants of the humbler classes, generally, this colony is under the highest obligation'.

Robert Lowe, speaking in the council, said:

'One person only in the colony has done anything effective – anything on a scale which may be called large – to mitigate this crying evil and national sin, and to fix *families* on our land . . . And strange to say, that one is a humble, unpretending, quiet-working *female* missionary . . . her mission is one of the most original ever devised or undertaken by man or woman; and the object, the labour, the design are all beyond praise.'

The gold-rush, which had made one branch of Mrs Chisholm's work no longer necessary, provided her, on her return to Australia, with a new field for her energetic philanthropy. She and her family sailed for Australia in April 1854 and landed at Port Phillip in July. A movement was begun to give her a public welcome, and at this function she spoke of the matters which were to claim the greater part of her attention while she remained in Australia.

## IX

The logical and necessary corollary of a family is a home. And Mrs Chisholm (who, of all people, must by now have known the minds of the poorer emigrants) insisted that the kind of home they wanted and should have was one 'of their own'. That is to say, they wanted land; and strangely enough, in this vast, unoccupied country, land was exactly what they found most difficult to obtain. Her opinion was strengthened by the visit which she paid shortly after her return to the diggings, and upon which she was accompanied by her eldest son. Hearsay was never enough for Caroline Chisholm; she must see for herself. To study the conditions in mining communities, to ascertain the state of the labour market, and to make arrangements for the reunion of 'diggers' with the families they had left behind, she undertook a journey, which must have been, for sheer discomfort, even worse than her journeys with the emigrant girls. The roads were indescribably rough, and there was no suitable accommodation on the way, so she slept 'in a waggon, under a dray, in the tents', always sustained and encouraged by the kindness and the appreciation with which she was greeted by the miners. 'The great and good Mrs Chisholm', said the *Bendigo Advertiser*, 'is applying the energies of her masculine mind to the subject of social reform among the diggings.'

On her return to Melbourne Mrs Chisholm lectured to a crowded hall upon her impressions of the diggings and pointed out that here again the lack of family life, the fact that the men, when their day's work was done, had nowhere to go and nothing to do but drink and quarrel, was fostering unhealthy and anti-social conditions. So that wives might be more easily enabled to join their husbands, she advocated the erection of sheltersheds along the route to the diggings, and again she insisted upon that necessary background for family life – the home.

'The great grievance of the diggers,' she said, 'is that they cannot get land. It is a grievance that requires to be immediately remedied. The diggers are a fine, intelligent body of men . . . their energy and activity are beyond anything I can express to you; and it is an unaccountable act of folly for the government to let the money these men earn be spent upon articles of foreign produce when they have the ground idle about them on which they could grow the same.'

Loud applause greeted these remarks, and she went on to say that when the people had comfortable homes 'the country will become a great country – and not till then'. Again and again she insisted upon the importance of fundamental things in the building of a happy and prosperous nation – homes, families, productive work, the cultivated soil. 'Let us fling to the wind this wild fallacy that public works carried on with borrowed money is fitting employment for newly arrived immigrants. Let us be wise in time and give to the people a fair scope for their activity . . . and we shall soon become a happy and contented people. We have become a nation of consumers instead of producers . . . if Sir Charles Hotham is a wise man, he will at once call to his assistance that first minister of finance – the plough.'

She did not feel, however, that because he had a little plot of land a man must necessarily become a farmer. The possession of land was to stimulate a sense of responsibility, a price of ownership, a feeling of independence, and to provide homes in which children could grow in health and security. 'What parent of thought,' she said once, 'can look on the crowded streets and witness the little children in the by-ways without feeling a desire to give them a healthier home, and one away from town dangers . . . Talk of compensations to squatters . . .' she adds, with one of her rare bursts of indignation, '. . . children ought to take precedence of sheep!'

But in the early months of 1857 the magnificent health and endurance, which had so long sustained her, broke down at last, and she was seriously ill. As soon as she was sufficiently recovered, she returned to the task of erecting sheltersheds along the route to Castlemaine. Tenders were called in April, and in due course, after the usual government opposition, the sheds were erected. Shortly after this Mrs Chisholm met with a serious accident, from the results of which she never entirely recovered. She lived quietly in Melbourne for some time, where one of her sons, now married, had his home, and then decided to move to the country. In the little village of Kyneton, near the head of the Campaspe River, the Chisholms lived until the year 1858, when, after another bout of illness, Mrs Chisholm decided to take a trip to Sydney with the younger children. The journey was perhaps too much for one only just convalescent, for in Sydney she suffered a relapse, from which she was slowly recovering when the children became ill, and in the same year her second son, William, died in Melbourne.

The family now made its home in Sydney again, Mrs Chisholm lecturing occasionally during 1859, 1860, and 1861, but unable to continue the active physical work of former years. In 1862 she wrote that she was beginning to suffer from the strain of 'hard work for many years . . . with late heavy domestic afflictions and severe bodily ailments.'

Not only these trials, but also financial difficulties, beset her at this time, and again, in spite of her failing health, she opened a school. This Educational Establishment for Young Ladies was situated first at Rathbone House, Newtown, and later at Greenbank, Tempe. In 1866, however, she decided to retire and return to England. On 22 September 1866, she arrived in her homeland, which she was not to leave again. In 1867 she was granted a pension of a hundred pounds a year, and for the next ten years she lived a retired life. She died in March 1877 and was buried at Northampton. Her husband survived her only for a few months.

X

That is the end of the story of Caroline Chisholm's life. The story of her work is still going on in hundreds of Australian homes, and we shall never quite know or fully appreciate its extent. Nor can we ever know, though there can be no harm in imagining, what she would think of us if she could return now.

In the various prophecies made during our first fifty years one word is noticeable, because of the regularity with which it crops up in estimates of our future 'greatness'. Even before the beginning of the nineteenth century, Sir Joseph Banks said: 'I see a prospect of empire and dominion that cannot now be disappointed. Who knows but England may rise again in New South Wales when she has sunk in Europe?' W. C. Wentworth, whose 'new Britannia in another world' echoes this thought, refers to Australia as 'Empress of the Southern Wave'. Governor Phillip speaks of 'laying the foundations of an Empire', and Campbell exclaims: 'Delightful land! in wildness ev'n benign,/The glorious past is ours – the future thine!/As in a cradled Hercules we love to trace/The lines of empire in thine infant face.'

Those were the early days of imperialism; the word and the idea had a spaciousness and a glamour that are beginning to be suspect. There are many in these troubled times who see in it one of the greatest obstacles to peace, and who feel that war is too high a price to pay for 'glory'. When we ask ourselves, as we must upon a hundred and fiftieth birthday, where we are heading as a nation, the story of Caroline Chisholm seems to point us, not to those dreams of 'empire' that were so freely predicted for us, but to a less spectacular and not unattainable goal, where we might repeat with truth and pride the words spoken by an Irish emigrant nearly a hundred years ago: 'This is a fine, plentiful country – there is no person starving here.'

# HELEN SIMPSON

## Australia is So Modern

Too old, a sanctuary of forgotten races
　　Whose unkind stars her pastures keep –
Now over secret, unattainable places
　　'Plane shadows scare the sheep:

Now to flat farms the eagle views as he poises,
　　That under heavy sun lie mute,
An airy impulse brings Prospero's island noises,
　　Sad Mariana's lute:

Impermanent as a scatter of wild birds fleeting
　　Above lost columns in the sand;
Child's voice flung at the mountain, echo repeating;
　　Rain on a statue's hand.

## Sesquicentenary: London, Sydney

The oak is a pool of time, growth widens through it
As from a stone dropped, imperceptibly rounding;
A hundred and fifty years, so many circles,
Widens the English city from groves not remembered.

Its nuts burst open by flame, the eucalyptus
Dies and renews, while men out of love with patience,
Scourging, trembling, conjure a town into being
Where once, no axe known, trees held safe congregation.

Growth in brief space, more swift than spring's running
　　grasses,
Growth exuberant, growth regardless of function,
Not to be checked, carrying something of terror –
Pang of a woman who halts, her hand at her bosom.

# FLORA ELDERSHAW

## A Group of Noble Dames

Between the work of Caroline Chisholm, in the early days of the colony, and that of Rose Scott there is a lapse of years, during which there was much pioneering work for women to do as individuals and as members of society. There was in those years, as ever, a great deal in the conditions of women and children, and of the helpless members of society, that called for succour and redress. There were women willing and able to do this work, to create practical organizations and found philanthropic traditions. It is impossible, in our narrow space, to enumerate all these pioneers, but it is possible to follow the policy of taking, perhaps arbitrarily, one figure or one group as a symbol or a representative, to give one clear story, instead of a survey of the whole, that must efface itself in a compression that would reduce it to a roll-call of names and dates.

The group that most aptly fills the years and weaves in the story of the women pioneers is that of the Windeyer women. For three generations they carried forward in different ways the work and cause of women in Australia.

The story of the Windeyer family in Australia is a very interesting one, and it is impossible to disentangle the story of the women from that of their menfolk, their husbands and fathers.

The Windeyers were of Swiss extraction, from Canton Berne, the William Tell country. The first to settle in England was a soldier, John William Windeyer, who arrived from Switzerland in 1735. His grandson, Charles, became a journalist, and was the first reporter recognized by the House of Lords. In 1805 he married Ann Mary Rudd, and in 1828 he came to New South Wales in the *Sarah*, with his wife and eight of their nine children. The eldest son, Richard, who was studying law, remained in England. Charles Windeyer had an honourable career in the colony, was chief clerk in the post office, a magistrate, and in 1840 first mayor

of Sydney. In 1836 his son Richard came out to join him. He had
followed in his father's footsteps as reporter in the House of Lords
and had been called to the Bar at the Middle Temple. He brought
his young wife, Maria, and their only child, William Charles.
At first everything went well. Richard Windeyer immediately took
his place as a leader of the Bar in Sydney. In 1843 he entered
the Legislative Council. About this time he bought a large estate
from Colonel Snodgrass, on the banks of the Hunter River, not
far from Newcastle, and named it Tomago, an Aboriginal word
meaning 'sweet water'. Here he cultivated the vine, cotton and
tobacco. Then bad times came; the depression that closed in during
the forties ruined him. He assigned his estate, and shortly after
died, broken-hearted, while on a visit to Tasmania. Maria was
left a widow, with a son of thirteen and no means. She was a
woman of spirit, and the last thing she intended was to sink into
genteel poverty. With the help and advice of her husband's friend
Robert Lowe, later Viscount Sherbrooke, she bought back part
of the Tomago estate, including the homestead, at the auction
in 1848. She set to work to make a success of wine-growing, and
she did. She was able to keep her son at The King's School and
then to send him to the newly opened university. She exhibited
her wines at the Paris Exposition of 1851 and got an award. There
is in the family archives a letter of congratulation from Napoleon
III on her achievement.

Meanwhile the young William Charles was fulfilling her
expectations and justifying any sacrifices she had made for his
education. He had a brilliant academic career and was the first
graduate in Arts of the University of Sydney in 1856. He was
called to the Bar in the following year, and shortly became crown
prosecutor. In 1859 he entered politics as member for Lower
Hunter. In 1870 he was solicitor-general in the Martin ministry,
and in 1877 attorney-general in the Parkes ministry. In 1879 he
became a judge in the Supreme Court, then senior Puisne judge,
an appointment which he held until just before his death in Italy
in 1897. He was a man of very liberal views, deeply interested
in education. He was vice-chancellor and then chancellor of the
university, a trustee of the Sydney Grammar School. He
advocated the higher education of women, and acted as chairman
of trustees of the Women's College in the University of Sydney.
He also gave his time and energy to many other public interests,
such as securing parks and recreation grounds for the people of

Sydney. In 1891 he had been knighted as an acknowledgment of his services.

Her husband's career and work provided a sympathetic medium for Lady Windeyer's character and abilities. Before her marriage she was Mary Elizabeth Bolton, the daughter of the Rev. Robert Thorley Bolton, of Padbury, Bucks, and of Hexham, on the Hunter River. Perhaps the ability and independence of Maria Windeyer led her son to seek the same qualities in his wife. This is certain, that Lady Windeyer would have been a pioneer and a leader in any society in which she had lived. She was a woman both gentle and forceful, sincerely charitable and able, because of the quality of her mind, to give form in practical institutions to her love of her fellows. Her husband's position, and the influential friends who gathered at their home, further enlarged her opportunities for well-doing.

The list of Lady Windeyer's activities is very impressive. In most of them she was not only a prime mover but a creator. Most of her efforts were directed towards the assistance of women and children in distress. She worked for the foundation of the Crown Street Women's Hospital, and was its first president of committee. She organized, in 1874, the Foundling Home in Macquarie Street, later the Ashfield Home for Babies. She suggested the boarding-out scheme for state children to Sir Henry Parkes. With Mrs Jeffries and Mrs Garran she originated the Boarding-Out Society, which later developed into the Children's State Relief Department, a great improvement on the herding together of children in institutions. She interested herself in education, especially of young children, and advocated the Froebel system. She gave her support to the Free Kindergarten Movement, and, in 1908, four years before her death, was president of the Newcastle Free Kindergarten. Among her other charitable works was the Ladies' Temporary Aid League, to help women in distress, and the Prison Gate Brigade.

Lady Windeyer's viewpoint included, not only women's needs, but also their rights. She was an indefatigable worker for womanhood suffrage, first as the president of the Womanhood Suffrage League of New South Wales, and then through the Women's Christian Temperance Union.

Archdeacon Boyce wrote of her sustained suffrage campaign:

'There was no window-smashing or bomb-throwing, no riot or disorder, no interference with meetings or attempts to intimidate Ministers of the Crown, but there was a vigorous agitation carried on upon ordered and constitutional lines, and successfully.

'Lady Windeyer was one of the heroines of the fight. She was a member of the Women's Christian Temperance Union that began it in the eighties and took to the end such a great part in the movement. In the early nineties she did much platform work in various parts of the state . . . She was logical, refined and sometimes very eloquent . . . One speech significant of her tact and readiness is vividly before my mind. It was a meeting at a spot on which political speeches were not allowed. A gentleman who had touched on politics by advocating votes for women was stopped and the next to speak was Lady Windeyer, but she reasoned round the question without referring to votes, so that her meaning became clear. She concluded amid much applause. She had made it plain by emphasizing the capacity of her sex that it was a hardship and a wrong that women were regarded as unfit for the franchise. She was a factor in moulding public opinion and so materially helped to prepare the way for the great victory.'

Her organizing ability was at the service of the community in other ways. She organized the Women's Industrial Exhibition of 1888, which provided funds for the establishment of the Queen Victoria Jubilee Fund, and she represented Australia upon the executive council of the Chicago World Fair, 1893.

As Lady Windeyer carried on the pioneering spirit of her mother-in-law in the social instead of in the individual sphere and gave her energies to the development of organized charities and endeavours, so her daughter, Miss Margaret Windeyer, carried it into still another field. She helped to pioneer the professions for women. As a girl she was an ardent suffragist and acted as recording secetary to Miss Rose Scott. Here she was following in her mother's footsteps, but she also had initiative. She was a new woman. She championed the feminine mind in a different but still practical way. She joined the Women's Literary Society and attended meetings at night. That was considered daring, and she had some difficulties with her family over it. She went further. She wanted to have a profession and earn her own living. She so far got her own way that she went to New York and attended the famous Library School there. She then worked as a volunteer in the Boston Public Library. Upon her father's death in 1897 she entered the Mitchell Library, Sydney, the first trained librarian in Australia.

Her private ambitions did not absorb all Margaret Windeyer's energies. She was largely responsible for the formation of the National Council of Women in Australia in 1896. She had brought the idea and even the design of the society back with her from America. Among her other social interests were the Bush Book Club, children's libraries, the Anzac Fellowship of Women, the Genealogical Society of Australia, the Women's College within the University of Sydney.

The Windeyer family has contributed to the legal life of Australia through five generations and three Windeyer women have made their mark upon Australian life.

# MILES FRANKLIN

## Rose Scott:
## Some Aspects of her Personality and Work

Over eighty years ago an exceptional child was growing up in a happy home at Glendon, on the Hunter River, near Singleton. Visitors were rare; she saw a shop only once in her first ten years, and that a travelling pedlar's cart. The child was a visionary and dreamer of dreams, and in the solitude of the Australian bush, the birds, the flowers, the dragonflies, the music of the swamp oaks and that of the river – so dearly loved as it gurgled over pebbles and boulders to lose itself later in the mystical sea – filled her thought and stimulated her imagination. At night the thrilling howl of the dingoes and the wail of the curlews had a message that was never to be lost. At ten years of age came a first visit to Grafton, which the child thought altogether wonderful. The daguerreotype of her at that time shows a being mature for her years with a face of appealing loveliness in which sensitiveness and strength are clearly evident. This was the little Rose Scott who had before her a long and influential life of public service.

Her grandfather, Dr Helenus Scott, of the East India Medical Service, was president of the Medical Board of Bombay and also Assay Master there. He was a friend and pupil of Jenner and the first to vaccinate in India. While there he was called to another province to attend a young military officer, Arthur Wellesley, with whom he formed a life-long friendship. After leaving India he had a practice in Bath, England. There his health failed and he was persuaded to come out to Australia. He and his sons, Robert and Helenus, chartered the ship *Britomart* and left for Sydney in 1820. The doctor died at sea and was buried at Capetown. The sons continued their voyage and arrived here in 1821. Helenus was offered a military career by his father's friend, who later became the Duke of Wellington, and set out to England to accept a cadetship, which was regarded as a prize, but at Valparaiso he learned that he was over age. He returned and the younger brother, David Frederick, went in his stead to Woolwich. Robert and Helenus worked in partnership at Glendon, where they had grants of land. Young men of large capital, they helped to develop the rural industries by importing seeds, plants and pedigreed cattle and horses. A horse named Dover, the most outstanding of their stables, had his portrait painted by Herring. The Scotts of Glendon speedily became an important family among the early squattocracy, or gentry, of New South Wales.

David, the Woolwich cadet, in the course of his career, was with Napoleon at St Helena, and later a captain in the Bombay Light Cavalry. He, too, in the end came to Australia, and married Maria, daughter of Colonel Barney, surveyor-general of New South Wales. Through the Indian connection was inaugurated the trade in walers, the famous army remounts.

In addition to Glendon the Scotts owned Dalkeith, renowned later for its merino stud. The Scotts were relatives of the Duke of Buccleuch and Earl of Dalkeith was the title borne by the eldest son, hence the naming of the station. Scott Street, Newcastle, and Scott Island also derive their names from the family.

Dr Helenus Scott's eldest daughter married Dr James Mitchell, and they were the parents of David Scott Mitchell, founder of the Mitchell Library. Helenus, the second son, born in Bombay, 22 May 1802, was married in the Chapel, East Maitland, on 2 September 1835 to Sarah Anne Rusden, daughter of the Rev. Geo. Keylock Rusden, MA, of Pembroke Hall, Cambridge, and the first government chaplain of East Maitland, where he laboured for twenty-six years. These were the parents of Rose. Canon Rusden, her grandfather, worked a great deal among the convicts and once when visiting a gaol after an uprising noticed the armed warders following him around. 'Why do you follow me?' he asked. When told that the convicts were in a bad mood and dangerous, he said: 'Go away; do not dare to follow me when I am about my Father's business.' The Canon also 'minded' the surplus cash of people in his district before the days of banks, and when the first bank was opened in Maitland was rewarded by a handsome present.

Two of the sons of this pioneer, uncles of Rose, made names for themselves as men of letters, one being Clerk of Parliaments in Victoria and a historian of Australia and New Zealand. Another was in the Victorian civil service and known as an exponent of advanced thought in days when young men read Tyndall, Huxley, Darwin, Mill, Comte and Spencer and debated their ideas in public. An aunt was the wife of Dean Selwyn.

Rose Scott was born on 8 October 1847, at Glendon, one of the elder members of a family of four daughters and three sons. The cultural influence of a childhood in the bush remained with her. She was spiritually rooted in her native land. She knew the pioneer activities. Her neighbourhood was visited by bushrangers. Her father and her uncle, Robert, organized a party and captured the Steel gang and handed them over to the Buffs, the regiment quartered in the district at the time. The Buffs allowed the men to escape. The Scotts, with superior bushmanship, recaptured them. The neighbouring settlers showed their appreciation by clubbing together and importing a silver service, which remains among the family treasures with the sword and epaulettes worn by Wellington's protégé, and the Wedgwood medallion of Wellington presented by the Duke himself to his friend Dr Scott.

In Rose Scott's girlhood the races were the liveliest social event of the year, and she retained one of the first books of rules of the Australian Jockey Club. One rule decreed: 'All dogs found on the course shall be destroyed.' The races were run for purses (of sovereigns), and Miss Scott preserved those won by her father's horses as far back as 1837, and one that was worked by the belle of 1842. Another treasure of the time was a myall whip handle carved by an old stockman of Glendon for her father, and a little dilly bag made for her from kurrajong bark beaten and then woven with colour. In those days the Aborigines surrounded her, and she found them most kindly. 'I loved all those dear people, and they loved me,' she would say when recalling her early days.

The Scotts were ruined financially by the failure of the Bank of Australia in the first big bank smashes of the 1840s. They could have recovered if given time and but for the extraordinary procedure of the government valuer of the day. Helenus Scott then had various official appointments, including warden of District Council and commissioner of Court of Requests at Patrick's Plains, collector of royalty at Louisa Creek, police magistrate at Carcoar, Wollombi, MacDonald River, and, finally, at Newcastle for twenty years. At Newcastle Rose lived with the family at 'The Barracks', and made long visits to her aunt, Mrs Selwyn. Following the death of her father in 1879 she and her mother moved to Sydney to live. Her first years there were occupied with the care of her mother and a brother-in-law with a nephew, who came to her upon the death of her sister when the child was an infant of two years. Mrs Scott died in 1896.

It is interesting to speculate why Rose Scott, sheltered by a more than ordinarily cultured and comfortable family life, should have developed into the inflexible crusader for the raising of the status of women and for every form of social justice. Genius is inherent, and sooner or later breaks from its chrysalis. Thus with Rose Scott. A number of her relatives were occupied with public issues, and she was sensitive to all suffering and injustice. While her young men friends were rejoicing in the plentiful sport to be had, she would be gathering the wounded birds in her pinafore, heart-broken and weeping at the cruelty and the waste of beauty.

But it was to Shakespeare that she attributed her entry into the lists in the cause of women and children. He early awakened her to 'passionate anger and indignation' in this matter. As she and her sisters sat at their needlework, Mrs Scott used to read aloud Shakespeare, William Tell, Sir Walter Scott and others. We have this in Rose's own words:

'When I was about seven years old my mother read to us *The Taming of the Shrew.* It was with suppressed indignation that I contemplated Katherine, at the bidding of her husband, taking off her cap and trampling on it! (I would have thrown it in his face!), and then her sermon (also at the bidding of her husband) to her sister Bianca and others upon the *duty of wives to their husbands!* "He is thy Lord, thy King, thy Governor, come, come you forward and unable *worms,* and place your hands below your husband's foot, in token of which *duty,* if he please, my hand is ready, may it do him ease!" When the reading was over I paced the garden, in a secluded spot, with clenched hands and fury in my heart! The craven wretch; to give in in that servile manner, and worse still to turn the tables on her own sex! From that moment I was a rebel against all injustice and wrong.

'I knew nothing of life, except the life in a happy and secluded home, illuminated by books. How I gloried in Vashti when I made her acquaintance, and as for Joan of Arc, I could never quite forgive either Shakespeare [for Katherine] or the English for their treatment of my *most beloved heroine.*

'The Crimean war, which I well remember, gave us Florence Nightingale – The Lady of the Lamp – heroine of commonsense and self-sacrifice, a real living woman, and so I gradually learnt that little good could be done in a world with dreams and visions *only*. Even then I must have been more than a dreamer. My mother taught us all to read at three years old, a little book kept by her shows this fact, and in a letter to my father she describes my interest in my lesson, the alphabet, the consonants, the very important vowels – and how I came to her afterwards and asked her what M T L spelt – F P Q – S T R – G M T. Was I trying at three years old to prove all things? – and did I view the poor consonants as helpless underdogs that needed righting . . .

'Time rolled on, and the bush home was no more. As I grew up I found that Charity was certainly necessary and to be worked for, but to give others what you would not like to accept yourself seemed rather unsatisfactory. The weeds might be clipped, but the roots were still in the ground, and again I felt, Justice alone could pull up the roots.'

Her first appearance in print on behalf of justice was a letter to the press, protesting against home lessons.

The most prominent of her activities was in the campaign for votes for women, which she entered in 1891. Manhood suffrage had been gained in 1858. In March 1891, Mrs Dora B. Montefiore invited a few people to her home in Sydney to discuss the formation of the Woman's Suffrage League. Those present were Mrs Wolstenholme, Dr and Mrs Elliot, Mrs Julian Ashton and the Misses Manning, Rose Scott and Margaret Windeyer. Rose Scott became corresponding secretary. At an early important meeting, Lady Windeyer, the president, had to be absent and insisted that Miss Scott should take her place. This Miss Scott did in great trepidation and was surprised to find that she had a voice and could think on her feet. This organization was wholly directed to the winning of the franchise for women in New South Wales. It had been preceded as far back as 1887 by the agitation of Mrs Euphemia Bowes, president of the Women's Christian Temperance Union. In 1890 the WCTU passed a resolution and set Mrs Pottie to found a Suffrage League, but 'many ladies refused to work under the auspices of the WCTU'. The matter lapsed for a time, but woman's franchise was one of the departments of work decided upon at the convention of the WCTU of 1891, and Mrs E. J. Ward (see her autobiography) became the first colonial superintendent of franchise in New South Wales. Sir Henry Parkes presided at the first public meeting of this department and brought the subject into practical politics in November 1890 (see *Hansard*) by introducing a bill to give the right to vote to all those of no legal disabilities 'without distinction of sex'. This bill did not reach a second reading. Among other pioneers of the measure, who continued to work for it, either in the Suffrage League or their own organizations, were Messrs Boyce, J. L. Fegan, G. D. Clark, Lady Windeyer, Mesdames Allen, Harrison, Jessie Dickie, Louisa Lawson and Annie and Belle Golding.

The first big meeting of the Woman's Suffrage League was in May 1891, its first resolution being moved by Professor MacCallum. In 1894 there was a general election, which was the opportunity for meetings in the city and suburbs and interviews with every prominent man of the moment. Circulars pleading the cause were sent to every candidate and deputations to politicians were a matter of course.

Thus Rose Scott gained experience under Lady Windeyer and welded her technique in public service. One of her first attempts was as a member of a committee to support Major Nield, MLA, in an effort to raise the age of protection for girls from fourteen to eighteen years. The bill was received in the Legislative Assembly with laughter. Rose Scott felt that if women had the vote they would be in a position to protect children and that such insulting conduct would be impossible.

She studied all arguments for and against votes for women and finally John Stuart Mill's *The Subjection of Women* made her an enthusiast. But progress was slow. Eleven years of many trials and set-backs were to pass till on 1 August 1902 the Women's Suffrage Bill was finally carried and added some 300,000 voters to the register. The federal constitution in 1902 conferred the vote for the federal parliament upon women as well as men. Women's state enfranchisement had preceded this in South and Western Australia, went through in Queensland in 1905, but in Victoria not till 1909. 'Not the laurel but the race,' was of fundamental importance. The campaign in its related activities was vital in awakening men and women to the possibilities of more expansive and ethical citizenship under courageous leadership in an era in Australian politics which gave zest to living here and drew the hopes and attention of peoples overseas.

Rose Scott considered votes for women the big nullah-nullah with which to attack laws and conditions unjust to women and children, but was too able to sink all her energies in its winning.

Prominent among concurrent campaigns was that for early closing. When women, and particularly young girls, had to toil in retail establishments from eight am to nine pm on week days, and until 11 pm on Saturdays, Rose Scott, the comfortably placed, never rested until these conditions were righted. She organized and addressed meetings and led or accompanied deputations to parliament or to religious assemblies and anywhere that help might be found. She called personally upon the owners of the big shops and tried to enlist their aid. The lord of one of the largest said that if Jesus Christ Himself came and asked him to close his shop early he would not do so. Many a weary shop girl and pale-faced shop assistant told the story of aching feet and dizziness in the sanctity of Rose Scott's drawing-room. They were first piloted there by J. D. Fitzgerald, who framed a petition which was signed by thousands of Sydneyites. There also among politicians came B. R. Wise and W. A. Holman to discuss a bill and to draft it on Miss Scott's rosewood table. The Early Closing Act of 1899 was the result, and its amendments of 1910, which are now all embodied in the Factories and Shops Amendment Act of 1936. Women inspectors in factories and shops, and sitting accommodation for all females employed there, are now realities which have come through the representations of Rose Scott.

She once said to an interviewer that Mr Hughes, with Mr Bavin, helped most to bring the Early Closing Act to fruition. 'In those days I used to bring the shop girls to my home on Sunday evenings. Poor girls, Sunday was their only free night, and I'd bring any politicians I could get hold of, or preferably their wives, to talk to the girls and get first-hand knowledge of their conditions, and what they wanted. I always said to would-be reformers, "Don't do things for people until you know what they want." I still believe in that motto, and think much more good could be accomplished if it were universally adopted. We got Sir William Lyne's sympathy because we induced Lady Lyne to come to my house and talk to the girls.'

She was shocked by the conditions surrounding the arrest of erring women – that they should be subjected to search by men, and to the ribald amusement of court officials. She busied herself and became lady president of the Prisoners' Aid Association, which endeavoured to help discharged women prisoners back to normal living, and thus carried forward the work pioneered by Mrs Gregory, of the great cricketing family. She succeeded in obtaining the appointment of matrons at the police stations, and was in part responsible for the provision of the early public lavatories for women in Hyde Park. Edmund Fosbery, inspector-general of police, so esteemed her that he gave her his card authorizing her 'to visit police watch-houses at any time'. She was much touched by a letter received from a woman of the streets, part of which was: 'We may be bad, but we are thankful, and it is a comfort to know that one woman thinks we are worth looking after.' In Rose Scott's own hand among her personal papers is this: 'One difference between men and women is that, at any rate, a woman knows when she is bad.'

The letters she received and those she sent must have totalled hundreds of thousands as experience took her along the way from the young lady who wrote her first letter to the *Sydney Morning Herald* in fear and trembling. Her correspondence was all done in her own hand, which aroused loving protest and even verses from those who found it difficult to decipher. The stamps came out of her own pocket. Her nephew, H. H. S. Wallace, often posted at midnight seventy-five or a hundred letters, and the tiny postbox had to be replaced by a pillar of adequate size. Even this piece of progress was attributed to the work of Rose Scott, as also the two seats for the public on lower Ocean Street.

Her inward mail was heavy with letters of appreciation from all kinds of people, with suggestions from the mighty, pleas for help, requests for advice, stories of success or happiness, anonymous missives of abuse, and a variety of weird proposals, all of which testified to the addressee's popularity and influence. One correspondent during the outbreak of the plague at the turn of the century stated his belief that any evil effects could be averted if Miss Scott would promenade on Pitt Street at a specified hour daily.

The story of the campaign for votes for women in New South Wales is the life story of Rose Scott from the 1890s onward, and through her as a focal point also preponderatingly the history of Sydney's intellectual and political life. It is instructive to recall what a furious opposition there was to anything now so normal as women's enfranchisement.

Rose Scott was ideally placed to sponsor the movement. She was of irreproachable family; no door was closed to her had society in the narrow import been her bent; she had means, not enough to be a snare and a burden, but ample to release her from worry concerning her present or future support. In his provision for her, her father anticipated Virginia Woolf in the estimate of five hundred pounds a year and 'a room of one's own' as indispensable to a woman to succeed in the arts. In addition, Rose Scott had beauty and charm. She was the personification of all that was most desirable and commendable in femininity. This must be stressed, for in Rose Scott's earlier decades woman's place was still the home in the restrictive sense. A woman who *did not* choose to marry was the target of slurs that she *could not*. A woman who wanted to develop her mental powers above those of a hen or a doll was *unsexed*. She was a warning to minxes who rebelled against the frowsy sentimentality that encrusted biological facts. The WCTU workers had met the charge that to demand votes for women was un-Christian and in defiance of the Bible. Rose Scott's womanly attractions were such that the most blatant males could not accuse her of *couldn't* in the matrimonial avenue. They could only moan that she *hadn't*, and what a loss it was to some man. In reply to an ill-natured remark of a state premier when she was on a deputation she was once roused to remark that she could have married had she chosen, but that was not the matter at issue.

She was always sensibly and graciously dressed for time and occasion, and her bonnets were the delight of Sydney. It was claimed by the wags that her complexion and bonnets did more than her arguments to win the vote. That was affectionate drollery. It is profitable to consider what enabled her to attract the best of every element in society and to make of social reform – sociology, that dismal science – an interest as vivid as that stirred by the arts or recreational association.

There was an intellect of unusual capacity behind her softly moulded features and pensively held eyelids, which gave a suggestion of sadness to an essentially wholesome face. Recalling her at the height of her maturity and power, she had the mind of a statesman, an astute tactician who could initiate, co-ordinate, convince, win love, command loyalty, and lead. Softly persuasive, in the end opposition receded before her more surely than from any impatient or more harsh attacks. To aid the keen mind was a wit quick but always tempered with sympathy for the other person's point of view. Carefully she would gather up the threads until politicians did her will, accepting her ideas as their own and reaping the political kudos. She had tenacity of mind and body to prevail over time and events. Her industry never flagged, her vision never failed in selfless purpose. Governments came and went, Rose Scott, like the personification of the woman's state, remained to influence them.

A woman in a million. She had a rich nature and a complex character, but the complexities were compounded into a satisfying harmony. A born warrior, she had no enemies because she was sincere and fair in opposition; manipulation of opposing factions to an end, expediency, was beneath her spiritual integrity; all her moves were logically thought out and backed by knowledge of life and conditions. Generous and philanthropic, she yet strove for results out of conviction of their justice rather patronizingly bestowing them out of charity. Essentially an aristocrat, she was broadly and practically democratic. She insisted upon being heard, and was heard, though she was not oratorical on public platforms, refused all offers of candidacy for parliament, and was firmly against the tactics of the militant suffragettes. She was not a fanatic or extremist, but always human and normal. 'The wretch,' she would sometimes say of a miscreant, in dulcet tones that softened the edge of rebuke. Had she been humourless and inconsequential of person her work could have reared itself like a monolith, worthy but unexciting, but elaborated and extended, as it was, by her genius for making a delight of association, a festival of friendship, her personality divided the honours with her achievements in political reform.

She was comfortable and happy in her home, and had zest in her housewifery, in which she said Bridget, her celebrated cook, collaborated with her. She brought the world to her home, which was said to be the most delightful place in Sydney. Her interests were so comprehensive that they were not above palmistry or telling character by handwriting. Her drawing-room was the only real salon that Sydney knew, and it alone would have made her famous. There public measures and social movements were encouraged or criticized, and public opinion clarified and shaped.

She was at home on Friday evenings, and on Saturday afternoons had an overflow meeting to give a chance to those who were getting on in years, or who had not enough years for late nights, or who lived at a distance. People went out to Edgecliff by tram, if not of the plutocrats who went by carriage or cab, and walked up the hill among the comfortable walled homes, which yielded glimpses of driveways under grand Moreton Bay figs, to fine Lynton, the famous two-storey cottage on Jersey Road, set in its thicket of bamboo, fuchsias, laurustinus, hibiscus, roses, camellias, and other shrubs and flowers. The cosy reception-rooms were often crowded. There came everyone of intellectual note or interest, residents or visitors to Sydney, regardless of clique, creed or political colour. There would be men in crumpled 'slops', who did not believe in evening dress, rubbing shoulders with dandies, to whom tails in the evening were a rite. Shy girls in high-necked frocks from the country or outer suburbs felt they were in high life as they chatted with some fashionable young person exhibiting every bare inch permissible in a gown that was the *dernier cri*. All were put at their ease, and found interest and companionship under the fusing influence of the hostess.

Young and ambitious men sought her for wise advice, weary politicians came for stimulation and sympathy, women came to her for help in their domestic or love problems or marital disasters. George Reid, Edmund Barton, William Lyne and B. R. Wise were frequent visitors. E. W. O'Sullivan, W. A. Holman, W. M. Hughes – the men in the early labour movement – were worshippers at her shrine. Ramsay Macdonald, the Webbs, Walter Burley Griffin, Dr David Starr Jordan, H. H. Champion, Sir William Windeyer, Sir William Cullen, Judge Docker, Judge Backhouse, Alfred Deakin, Frank Cotton, James Ryan and John Longmuir, John Quick, B. E. Minns, E. Phillips Fox and Frank Fox, Fred Johns, Hugh J. Ward, Mrs Molyneux Parkes, Vida Goldstein, the Garrans, the Davids, the Franklins, Olga Morgan (Mrs Bradbury), Louisa Macdonald, of the Women's College, Harriet Newcomb and Margaret Hodge, the founders of Shirley, Miss Florence S. Wearne, the doyenne of women in the state public service, were some of the many names to be found in Rose Scott's card bowl.

She knew Henry Kendall, Victor Daley, Henry Lawson, Bertram Stevens, Barbara Baynton, Jeanie Gunn, Ada Holman, Zara Aronson, Bernard O'Dowd, A. B. Paterson, Mabel Forrest, Francis McKenna, A. A. Bayldon, Sidney Partrige, Annie Rentoul, L. Hopkins ('Hop'), E. J. Brady, Laura Bogue Luffman, Sydney Jephcott, A. H. Chisholm, E. J. Dempsey, Essex Evans, Nina Murdoch, and many another who paved the way of Australian authorship, and treasured letters from them. To her went the first copy of the memorial edition of John Farrell's poems. Politicians felt she was particularly their colleague, absorbed in issues of state: literary aspirants felt equally that their efforts and personalities were of first concern to her, because she had a vital appreciation of Australian art and literature. Till the last writers sought her.

The Anglican, Roman Catholic, Presbyterian and Methodist clergymen of her parish all visited her. She would tell her friends that she was a renegade descendant of the clergy, her maternal grandfather being a canon of the Church of England, her uncle Dean Selwyn, and her brother-in-law Canon Bowyer Shaw. Miss Scott said that all three were men that even their relatives could respect. Regarding the rank of the clergy, she declared that a curate should live in a palace and a bishop in a gunyah, on the principle that the deeper the man got into his calling the more humble and Christ-like his attitude and mode of living should be, and that the test for advancement should be the alacrity with which the curate would exchange the palace for the gunyah. She maintained that she had her own private religion, but could respect all other creeds, and held that Mazzini and Jesus Christ were two of the greatest men who ever lived. She knew Cardinal Moran, and admired his intellectual attainments but not his propensity for fighting. She was associated with Archbishop Kelly in her work for the prisons, and spoke of him as a worthy exponent of religion with the kindly tongue of the typical Irishman.

The hours at her evenings were often very late. People were loath to bring inspiring and witty talk to an end, where every subject could be discussed, but no gossip. William Lane, before he left for his New Australia in Paraguay, would pour out his dreams and plans until two am; Lawrence Bradbury, of London *Punch*, called early on the way to an official ball, but returned near midnight, and lingered until the small hours began to grow. Guests voiced the most learned or the most unorthodox views. A new-thoughty American visitor of the Elbert Hubbard vintage wrote in his hostess's autograph album, 'God is an empty tablet on which stands that which we have written.' This drew a later entry: 'Mr Hanks's God may be exactly what he says, but there is an author for all the wonders of the universe; and I call that author, not an empty tablet, but God. (Signed) G. H. Reid.' An afterthought was added: 'My dear Miss Scott. Excuse this difference of opinion. All your friends agree on one point – we love you. GHR Aug. 10, '09.'

Her home was the haven of the poor and dispirited, as well

as the rallying-ground of the intellectuals. All who knocked at the hospitable door received attention or aid. Despite drunkenness being abhorrent to her, she would mix a pick-me-up for an inebriate, while pointing out to him the error of his ways. One strapping fellow was an exception. He demanded money while 'under the influence'. Miss Scott told him he looked well able to support himself. He began to argue, then to bully, and finally threw a piece of piping through the glass door. With the aid of a housemaid he was routed. Miss Scott demanded of a carter, who had been near at hand, why he did not protect a lady. He explained that he thought the abusive one was Miss Scott's husband, and that he was careful never to interfere between husband and wife. Miss Scott would relate such incidents without stressing the point and with a humorous laugh. She felt that men were merely naughty children who should be mothered on to a more adult plane, thus under her own thinking power realizing the unrefuted theory of Lester F. Ward, that woman is the racial stem and man a variant – a mere experiment.

In one of those confession books – less flippant than customary – which were the fashion of her day, Rose Scott made characteristic entries: The true place of women in society, she wrote, was 'Not beside man, but just in front of him. "The woman soul leadeth us on".' Matrimony was described as 'Friendship under difficult circumstances.' The qualities she most respected in men and women were 'Strength – moral and physical, and in woman the courage to be herself.' The characters she admired most in real life: 'Women who add to their own virtues those of men: men who add to their own virtues those of women.' A brief definition of love, 'The highest friendship.' Her idea of happiness: 'To forget all about happiness.' She would 'redress the wrongs of children'. Reforms advocated were: 'All which are included in the freedom of the individual (soul and body).' Her favourite Christian name: 'That of the first Christian.' The noblest aim in life: 'To break the chains of captives and make the Ideal the Real.' Her ambition: 'To do some good in the world, and no evil, no harm.' Flowers, birds and beasts asked the playful book, but Rose Scott in 1899 wrote seriously, 'Birds in freedom, not cages; beasts, not of the zoo or working for wages.'

In addition to the political activities mentioned, she was president of the Ladies' Associated Swimming Clubs of Sydney, so long as their exhibitions were not open to men spectators. (She strongly resented the female form being exploited in the advertisement of wares on public hoardings and elsewhere.) She was one of the first consulted by Dr Mary Booth when founding the Women's Club, and held office as a vice-president until her death. She was on the ladies' committee to raise funds to build the Women's College at the university. Later she was president of the Wattle Club, founded to foster native sentiment. She was identified with Testators' Family Maintenance and Guardianship of Infants (1916) and the Woman's Legal Status Act (1918), as well as the establishment of children's courts and the segregation of the unfit. She was a freetrader and always non-party and non-sectarian. She was against state borrowing and the federation of Australia, and favoured direct taxation, old-age pensions, and land and income taxation.

Comparable with the position of Rose Scott in Sydney was that of Catherine Helen Spence in Adelaide. Miss Scott had unbounded affection and admiration for her contemporary, but it was not until 1900 that Miss Spence came to Sydney and stayed with Miss Scott. Miss Spence was then seventy-five and Miss Scott in her fifty-third year. An old acquaintance has recorded that they called each other by their Christian names as unaffectedly as girls, and found much enjoyment in the visit. Miss Scott had a special evening for practice in the Hare-Spence system of voting. Among those who took part were Sir William McMillan, Messrs Walker, B. R. Wise, Jas. Ryan, J. Longmuir, A. J. Gould, Bruce Smith and W. A. Holman. Miss Spence stated that this evening paved the way for the success of her big public meeting on the same subject two days later, when the attorney-general took the chair.

Rose Scott always reminded those eager to help social reforms that it was necessary to gather first-hand information of conditions. Speaking of her own methods, she said, 'The Benevolent Asylum, Police Courts, Lock-ups, Gaols had to be visited, and though this experience was often loathsome and terrible, one had to remember the story of Mrs John Stuart Mill and her daughter, to whom she told some sad truths. "Oh mother," said the daughter, "I cannot bear to hear of such things!" "My child," replied the mother, "what other women have to endure you at least can bear to hear of."'

In the cause of woman suffrage she travelled and gave lectures in New South Wales, Queensland and Victoria, in which she urged women to vote for decent men and good measures, and to avoid party politics and sectarianism. She gave her services free, and only for long distances accepted anything for her train fares. When the women of New South Wales had the vote both in the state and federal parliaments she was asked to make a political forecast, which she did in *Table Talk* in March 1903:

'What is the Australian woman going to do with her vote . . . Who is to guide woman? I reply: Certainly no man, in the first place! Man, with his pitfalls of extravagance, outward show, Party Government, sectarianism, war, and all other follies! No. In the first place – woman must be guided by her own conscience and her wonderful perceptive powers. Secondly, by her fellow-women, who have so long studied matters political – from the woman's point of view. Thirdly, we shall be glad to learn what many men among us can teach – but it is not every man who *thinks* that he can teach, who is worthy to be chosen as a mentor. Here, again, must woman use her perception and reason. The chief guide is always to be found *within, not without*. We must, in fact, *think* for ourselves.'

She continued regarding the earnestness and humility of women towards their new responsibility – the sacred duty to use it wisely. She saw in lesser women some reflection of herself – women as they could be, exceptional women, rather than average women as they were. What might be her point of view now, when women as well as men in large numbers are brought to the polling boths only to escape a fine, and when among these are to be found some of her old-time crusaders, who have arrived at this state of political indifference through thinking for themselves and observing the nullification of parliamentary power by the party system?

But days of such parliamentary decadence were not yet.

The League for Woman Suffrage was disbanded. Rose Scott had held office continuously and without opposition from its beginning – the only officer to do so. She reorganized her forces in the League for Political Education – non-party and non-sectarian. She continued her platform work. Her platform manner had a misleading simplicity because of endearing hesitancies in expression, which gave a conversational character to her utterances. She was never hortatory or vehement. She did not antagonize her hearers: she disarmed them. An idea of her style can be gained from a lecture on the political education of women, delivered under the auspices of St Matthew's Literary and Debating Society at Windsor in 1904:

'It is also well to see both sides of this question, and to remember that it is an evil thing for any class or sex to have complete control over any other class or sex. "There is no instance on record," says Buckle, in his great history of civilization in England – "there is no instance on record of any class possessing power without abusing it." Kings, nobles, property-owners, owners of slaves (black and white), when possessing unlimited power over others, became tyrannical and abused their power; and so we see that the laws of most civilized nations especially depress and degrade women . . .

'Remember, I do not mean every individual man is a tyrant, but I speak of man as typifying the power that rules; and that, my friends, is the crux of the whole affair. The power that rules! There can be no ideal, no lofty conception of either a home or a nation if in either home or nation there is no ideal of and development of self-government . . .

'Take the home, which is often called, and really is, the foundation of the life of a nation. If the parents allow their boys to dominate their sisters, to have the best of everything at meals, the best rooms in the house, the best places and chairs, and to rule over the sisters entirely, even in games, what are the results? The boys naturally consider themselves first, and are oftentimes tyrannical bullies. The girls, meek and servile to the boys, generally quarrel among themselves. They live to please the boys, who have the power to rule the house, and they are disloyal to each other. This, on a larger scale, is a picture of a very great part of our national life . . .

'Mazzini said, "Laws framed only by a single fraction of the citizens can never, in the very nature of things, be other than the mere expressions of the thoughts, aspirations, or desires of that fraction . . .

'Some people are so terrified of anything which implies change, never mind what that change may be. In 1790 it was considered a shocking innovation to appoint women as schoolteachers in America. When Sir Samuel Romilly proposed to abolish the death penalty for stealing a handkerchief, the law officers of the Crown said it would endanger the whole criminal law of England! When the Bill abolishing the slave trade passed the House of Lords, Lord St Vincent rose and walked out, declaiming that he washed his hands of the ruin of the British Empire. People have even protested against steamers, saying they were contrary to nature! At the close of the reign of Charles II there was a fierce opposition to street lamps – as there always is to fresh light – (*laughter*) – and in the reign of Queen Elizabeth the working people were actually forbidden by law to use forks, as it was considered it would make them too presumptuous to have the use of that which was useful to and in a sense belonged to the aristocracy.' (*Laughter*)

Rose Scott liked to recall parliament as it was in the lively days of women's demand for the vote. 'Just imagine such men as Mr Reid, Mr Haynes, Mr Hughes and Mr Wise all in one house. In those days parliamentary sittings were an education and an entertainment. All four had such wit — Reid so ready with repartée, Haynes so infectiously humorous, Hughes so cuttingly sarcastic, and Wise so scintillatingly brilliant. Contrasting the cleverness of those days with the abuse that has passed for smartness in late parliaments, we who enjoyed the flow of wit only begin to understand now how privileged we were.' She treasured the telegram which Sir William Lyne sent her when the suffrage bill was passed, and esteemed the work of Sir John See, who was for the measure when wily politicians knew its advocacy would do themselves no good. She thought highly of J. C. Watson, and was mystified by his retirement from politics, which she considered a blow to the Labor Party. She took pleasure in one of W. A. Holman's lectures at the Socialist Club. 'He looked inspired, and I doubt if I have ever heard anyone more eloquent.' She added: 'Of course, Mr Holman had the advantage of a beautiful voice and great charm of manner, while Mr Reid [she always called him Mr Reid] and Mr Hughes were eloquent in spite of their voices.' In her opinion Bishop Moorhouse was as arresting a speaker as Mr Holman, and Alfred Deakin the best speaker that she ever heard.

Rose Scott did all things without seeming haste or over-crowding. No one seeking her aid or sympathy felt she had anything more important claiming her attention. Her methods and manner were leisurely and gracious, those of the well bred before speed and noise and mechanized entertainment abolished repose. To the last she attended to a long Christmas list, for which the least memento was chosen with understanding of the donee. Her immense range of interests and activities shows what one woman can accomplish if freed from financial and domestic restrictions. She was a product of her time, when a personality could develop and hold its own like a tree, and not be smothered in the successive crops of notorieties forced into prominence by hot air, and withering like grass as soon as the artificial sustenance is withdrawn. She belonged to humanity at large, and as the richest universality is autochthonously rooted, Rose Scott was ardently, self-respectingly Australian, and loved her country from the bone outward. She never left her native shores. Some have said that this resulted in a certain limitation of her outlook. These commentators sometimes exposed their own limitations, but in a state so colonial that all its bright lights go abroad for larger scope, and its strong young men seek adventure in imperial wars, it is interesting to speculate what effect a deep acquaintance with life in other countries would have had on Rose Scott's Australianness. Possibly but to confirm and deepen her perspective.

She had the Australian delight in poetry, and herself wrote verse and a few short stories, but whatever literary gifts she had were diverted into and exhausted by correspondence. She enjoyed humorous rhymes, and some of her limericks were illustrated and printed in the *Bulletin*.

> There was a young man of blue blood,
>     Whose ancestors swam in the Flood,
> But his lofty repose dwelt most in his nose,
>     And a tree grown in ancestral mud.
>
> There was a young lady of fashion,
>     Who for everything chic had a pashion,
> Thought it vulgar to vote, yet for hours would glote
>     On the last way of tying a sashion.

These two lines occur in a poem to the memory of Mrs Julian Ashton:

> The day in sunrise lives, in sunset dies,
>     And on the joy of life the shadow lies.

Rose Scott was herself the subject of poems, and treasured those written to her by Mary Gilmore and Louisa Lawson. She honoured Louisa, the mother of Henry, as one of Australia's greatest pioneers in women's emancipation and as her own fore-runner and colleague. Her friendship with the Lawson family included three generations.

With time she left to younger people the cause of women and children on the foundations which she had so soundly laid and with her standard still aloft. This released the best thought of her last years to the forwarding of internationalism through the International Council of Women. She advocated the consolidation of women's ideals throughout the world, especially to bring peace among the nations, and in the New South Wales branch of the London Peace Society found work that was dearest of all to her heart. She was the founder of the organization in 1907, and remained its president until failing health forced her to resign in 1917. In the days of the Boer war she maintained the opposing point of view, to which the world came later. Her pronouncements in those days on the necessity for peace and freedom, and on the dangers of inflated imperialism, remain necessary warnings and sane guidance. No one in Australia had been more constantly or more popularly reported in the press than Rose Scott, but during the European world war complete silence reigned on her efforts towards peace. She remained true to ideals of peace, and with other steadfast colleagues, like Mesdames Wearne, Harwood, Bonney, and the Rev. A. Rivett, continued to press the cause.

The European war was an abrogation of all her ideals. Advancing years and growing deafness drove her back upon the past and into her garden. Her garden was a perpetual delight, a bird sanctuary for wily silver eyes, doves, blue wrens, swallows and sparrows. She found time to tie up little parcels of fuchsia and geranium cuttings to drop in the streets, for she said that people finding a parcel would think the cuttings precious and give them a home in their gardens. Even her peccadilloes (if any) and her idiosyncrasies had originality and charm.

In thanking a friend for a booklet of the Northern Rivers received during the war, she referred to the trees and plants which Grafton owed originally to her uncle, Dean Selwyn.

'I did love that booklet you sent me. The old place I knew so well! Imagine my first visit to Grafton, in 1857, at ten years of age – the lovely trees all along the riverbank, the purple and white ipomeas decorating the trees. The loveliness of it! I never forgot my next visit, ten years later, to my uncle and aunt Selwyn – so much of the beauty gone, and banana trees everywhere . . . yes, I rode from Grafton to Gordon Brook, and then on to Yulgilbar Castle. I can see my window in the picture. A bat came one night to visit me, and it was hard work to get it out.'

A year later she wrote to the same friends:

There is nothing that so completely takes one away from all the present world horrors as flowers and plants and their beauty and wonders.

'One wonders if this murderous war will go on for years, or what will happen. Negotiation would be better than exhaustion or annihilation; and yet the rulers of Germany seem to be criminal lunatics, who cannot be reasoned with. It is like a huge fire – you see it destroying everything, animate or inanimate, and you are powerless to help. It is strange, that those who have been at the war from the first get no notice, no honours, while those who go for a few months come back and get decorated and praised – the way of the world, I suppose. The meek, and those who cannot push themselves forward, may inherit the earth, but its honours all seem to go to those who are anything but meek.'

Every letter to friends at that time breathed sorrow and sympathy for the waste of the flower of manhood.

Rose Scott's final public service was as an officer of the International Council of Women. Upon her retirement in 1921 her friends made her a presentation of money, which, public-spirited to the last, she used to found a prize for a woman law student at the University of Sydney. Her friends, upon the suggestion of Miss Wearne, also subscribed to have her portrait painted by Longstaff. She consented, on condition that the portrait should go to the National Art Gallery, where it now hangs.

Of this she said wistfully, why did they not paint her when she was young and beautiful? But she was beautiful from childhood to old age, as her portraits and the memory of those who behold her testify. At the unveiling of this Longstaff portrait by Lady Forster on 22 September 1922, Miss Scott made one of her last public utterances. She was now failing in strength, and had undergone the long and heart-breaking ordeal of the war, but in her remarks, falling as lightly and fragrantly as rose petals, was the old glint of wit and the thought or sentiment to lift her hearers into the upper air:

'Long ages ago, when I admired Henry Lawson's picture in the Gallery, I used to say none should ever paint me but Mr Longstaff – little thinking that my wish would ever come true. And indeed I must pay tribute to Mr Longstaff for all his patience and courtesy. For when I first went to him, I had been very ill. Then came summer, with its glorious sunshine, bluebirds and dragonflies, and I most aggravatingly became ten years younger! At any rate, he painted a Rose Scott that cannot make speeches, or argue upon every subject in Heaven or earth – silence being an excellent gift in a woman – and *this* Rose Scott, being a restless being, found it very hard to sit still – and so she moved the only thing she could move, and that was her tongue.

'It has been said by a great writer: "That the end of life is a journey among ruins!" Well, my friends, we all have our Gethsemanes, our losses and sorrows, and if our hearts embrace all humanity in our own dear country and in the world, the last few years have brought many ruins. But in my own case, and I am sure in many others, the beautiful ivy of friendship covers many ruins. What affection is there so deep, so lasting as a friendship? Love without wings it has been called.

'In all other relations of life, unless there is the spice of friendship, how insipid and often antagonistic they become. Make chums of your children, pals and mates of your husbands and wives, brothers and sisters, and those you employ, and at once we see this glowing opal entering into the common ore of life, and all relationships are transfigured.

'We Australians are a great people for Liberty, for wide spaces and deep silences, and friendship typifies all these. So you would see how hard it is for me to thank you, as I would like to do, for this priceless gift of friendship, which is the origin of any honours you have conferred upon me.'

Among the faces she missed from the gathering she spoke of 'Mr Archibald, of *Bulletin* fame, that most benevolent Mephistopheles'. Also, 'My nephew, my chum from his babyhood, regrets as much as I do his absence in Melbourne, but writes with his usual humour that he hopes I will make a tactful speech and beg people not to think I am really as bad as I am painted.'

It was in the rearing of her nephew, H. H. S. Wallace, that Rose Scott had the joy and responsibility of practical motherhood and a companion with a lively sense of humour, which, to preserve a balance, is more necessary in social reform than in any other sphere of activity.

This last speech, with the dragonflies and bluebirds, was consonant with the little dreamer in the bush long ago and the lovely old lady with silvery hair walking among her flowers, who could say, 'You never know when there may be a fairy sleeping between the petals.'

Her last days made demands upon her courage that medical science was powerless to avert, and which the loving care of her nephew, H. H. S. Wallace, and her niece, Rose Scott Windon, and many faithful friends could do little to soften. She died on 20 April 1925. She was a founder of the Cremation Society, and at her wish was among the first to be cremated. Her ashes went back to her beloved bush. A tree was planted at Rookwood to commemorate her.

A great personality, a distinguished and gallant woman.

## The Woman of the House

O, restless woman, woman of the house,
your footsteps echo
to and fro
up to the windows,
down to the door
on the naked floor . . .
They sound like a rosary
told fitfully
on wooden beads . . .
What area your needs,
O restless woman, woman of the house?
There is a fire on the hearth, love in the house . . .

Hush . . . there is a high wind
in the dark trees
and a voice in the wind . . .
The brown leaves run past the door,
they sound like the feet of a child.
The night has thrust fingers of wind
beneath the closed door,
they have stolen the peace
from my heart . . .
I cannot be still . . .
There is a voice in the wind
and a soul in the night . . .
O, I have not the peace in my heart
to be still by the fire . . .

# WINIFRED BIRKETT

## Some Pioneer Australian Women Writers

*I*

We cannot review any pioneering work done in Australia without being reminded that the colonial spirit was, naturally and not undesirably, a self-conscious one. So self-consciousness, proud or deprecatory, shot with the power of astonishment or complacently refusing to be surprised, is in all our first excursions into literature. We see the woman writer in particular as being very keenly aware of the pregnant age and the romantic environment in which she found herself; and when she came to record her observations, or to make them, together with the colour of her own experiences, a background for fiction, out of this peculiar sensibility to time and place, she wrote, not for Australian generations coming after, but for English contemporaries. Those 'at home' must be informed of a strange country and one of the conditions under which colonists lived and had their singular being. The incentive to write must then have been tremendous, and nearly every woman of education at one time or another kept a 'journal'. Perhaps publishers were only discreet in doling out such rewards as they paid to Catherine Spence: their offices and markets might otherwise have been flooded with inky manuscripts from a young colony trying, after the manner of youth, to impress its elders and reconcile itself with the fact of its own bewildering existence.

Catherine Helen Spence, of whom we have just spoken, was not among the native-born. In 1839 she came to Adelaide from Scotland, she being then just fourteen years of age and the city of her adoption less than three. She had been born in Melrose, the romantic village on Tweedside, only two miles distant from Scott's famous estate of Abbotsford. She explains in her autobiography that members of her family never came into actual contact with Scott, because he was a conservative, although her father (a lawyer) and her grandfather (a medical practitioner) represented opposing reformist interests; in that day and place political loyalties involved much, and though she always regretted her lost opportunities of acquaintance with Scott, not anywhere does she deplore the reasons for their loss; well did she support her reformist family's principles and maintain its ardour in her own generation! But she was intimate enough with Scott's written memorials of the districts so dear to them both, and one of the memories she brought with her to Australia was of the great writer's impressive funeral moving through the lovely countryside of the Scottish border to Dryburgh Abbey, where many of the Spence family had been buried.

Her parents had married three months after the Battle of Waterloo, and Catherine was born into a tremendously changing world. She was not too preoccupied, through the smaller and more intimate affairs of a happy childhood, to note the significance of happenings going on about her, or to regard in a merely personal way those country-wide changes which reacted more directly upon herself and her home. Politics must always have been a keen interest in that household, for she mentions having been taken, wrapped in a cloak, to hear an anti-conservative agitator from Edinburgh speaking at the local market cross – an occasion evidently considered important enough to demand the attendance of a small girl just recovering from measles.

She went to a local school for gentlewomen, kept by a Miss Phin, where the education dispensed must have been more thorough and various than was usual in small seminaries a century ago, and there she developed and nursed an ambition to become 'a teacher first and a great writer afterwards'. This ambition received its first setback when her father found it impossible to honour his promise of sending her to Edinburgh to finish. In 1839, after a long series of bad investments, he was finally and completely ruined by speculation in the wheat market. Any financial recovery in Scotland was impossible, and it was decided that, with only five hundred pounds capital advanced by the mother of Mrs Spence, the family should emigrate to the new settlement of South Australia and begin again. As it turned out, the father himself was to profit nothing by the move, and in a few years he died of a 'decline'; but Catherine and the rest of the family, bringing to the new land in the beginning all the best and most serviceable attributes of the Lowland Scot, eventually found success and happiness there.

The total change of climatic conditions possibly saved Catherine's life. A sister of sixteen and another two years old had already died of consumption, and there had been indications, before they left Scotland, of Catherine herself being 'far gone in the national complaint', as Stevenson has put it. For some time, however, the recovery of her health seemed to be all the good fortune she met with in Adelaide. Depression settled upon the family from the moment of their coming ashore. In spite of the eulogies of its advertisers, a first view of the new settlement was not prepossessing. Catherine says she might have echoed the words of Robert Thomas, founder of the Adelaide *Register*, in like situations: 'When I saw the place at which we were to land, I felt inclined to go and cut my throat.' On a log in Light Square she sat down and wept, as she waited for her father to fetch the key of a house in Gilles Street, which was to be their temporary dwelling.

It was early summer and drought-time when they arrived, and in such a season, the Spences were afraid to begin the cultivation of the eighty-acre plot of land they had previously acquired. They remained near the town. Leaving the raw wooden house of their first habitation, they bought a large marquee and pitched it on Brownhill Creek, above where Mitcham now stands. Then they bought fifteen cows and a pony and cart, and vended milk in the town for a shilling a quart. In this manner the family lived for seven months, their diet consisting largely of rice, of which they had bought a ton cheap. At the end of that time they moved their small dairy to West Terrace, Adelaide, and shortly afterwards the father got the position of town clerk at a salary of one hundred and fifty pounds a year, a small enough advance in prosperity, as the rent of their new premises was seventy-five pounds. Even this, however, did not last long, for the new city was not yet capable of supporting the luxury of a municipal corporation, and its premature scheme of local government collapsed.

Through this position of her father's Catherine got her first insight into electoral methods. Rowland Hill was then secretary to the Colonization Commissioner for South Australia, and he had drawn up the Municipal Bill, introducing therein a clause that provided for proportional representation at the option of the ratepayers. This provision was unique at the time, and Catherine was to remember its peculiar significance some twenty years later, when she began her crusade on behalf of what she called 'effective voting'.

If the little band of doctrinaires who first settled Adelaide found life there hard enough in material respects, they were not without mental interest and stimulus, and local society, if restricted, was at least congenial. They may have felt sometimes that they lived intellectually by taking in each other's washing, but, to extend the metaphor, it was not a washing of such poor quality as to be quickly worn out. Older people, transplanted too late, may sometimes have found only disappointment and discontent, but the younger generation there felt the excitement and the satisfaction of the making of the place. Catherine says: 'We took hold of the growth and development of South Australia and identified ourselves with it.'

But still one needed a little money, or some remunerative occupation, even for the enjoyment of such a life as this, and Catherine admitted that the two or three years following her arrival were the most unhappy of her life. Towards the latter part of that time she began to write: an occasional letter to the *South Australian* and some verse gave her the gratification of seeing herself in print at an age when this could give her the keenest thrill. But as yet, with no fund of matured experience to draw upon, and with any immediate exploring of the ways of life restricted by poverty and her own shyness, she had only the most inadequate material to her writer's hand. She could not have failed to realize this, and it must have added to her adolescent sense of frustration. Neither did she possess the essentials of the purely imaginative writer, and her talents were more analytical than intuitive from the very beginning. It became necessary, then, for the life of her authorship, as well as for her own independence, to mend her poverty in some way. She resolved to find a post as daily governess, if it meant no more than sixpence an hour; and actually for this pay, when she was seventeen, she went to teach the combined families of the postmaster-general, the surveyor-general, and the private secretary. This gave her an income altogether of five shillings a week. Afterwards she may have found an occasional pleasure in seeing herself in print, but the fact of bringing five shillings a week regularly into a penurious household was a deep and abiding satisfaction.

She continued to teach for some years, and meanwhile wrote what she could. Her sister had married Andrew Murray, who had taken over the *South Australian*, and he continued to give her work grudging admission to that paper's columns. Later on Murray joined the staff of the Melbourne *Argus*, and then he left the other paper partly in the charge of Catherine; but funds ran out, and it could not be kept going more than a few months after he had abandoned it. About this time the goldrush to Victoria set in, and South Australia became emptied of its men. Catherine wrote her first novel with this event as its theme, and William Bakewell, who contributed the preface, put the strange situation of the colony in these words:

'Finding the gold would not come to them, the people determined to go to the gold. Accordingly the entire male population, with comparatively few exceptions, removed in the course of a few short weeks to the vicinity of Mount Alexander and Forest Creek . . . The exodus was almost complete, and entirely without parallel in the history of any country . . . In those days there was no king in Israel, and every woman did what was right in her own sight . . . None but women and children were to be seen anywhere, and the skill manifested by them in the management of affairs was the subject of much admiration. The entire vintage of that year was gathered and the wine made by them; and never was there better made . . . A state of society unsung by poets, and such as was never seen before, existed, in which gentleness and courtesy and loving kindness reigned, and which will never be forgotten by those whom a supposed hard fortune compelled to remain behind. Had Mr Tennyson been there at the time another book might have been added to his *Princess*.'

This book of Catherine's was called *Clara Morison*, and it is now regarded as the first good Australian novel. It was published anonymously in 1854 by J. W. Parker & Son, having previously been declined by Smith Elder & Co. with the stereotyped comment that the author could do better. The publishers bought the copyright for forty pounds, from which they deducted ten pounds as a fee for abridging the MS. Her second book, *Tender and True*, was bought by Smith Elder & Co. (She seems to have persisted in a fancy to be accepted by the publishers of Charlotte Brontë.) They paid her twenty pounds, and the book ran through three large editions. After all, governessing at sixpence an hour did not compare so unfavourably with the writing of two-volume novels.

When she was twenty-five she gave up teaching altogether and concerned herself more with writing and with those public questions which were presently to claim her much more fully. For some time she acted as Adelaide correspondent to the Melbourne *Argus*, but women were not *persona grata* in journalism in those days, and she signed her letters with the name of her brother John. She received fifty pounds a year from the *Argus* for this deception, and it came to an end when the telegraph rendered any more measured correspondence obsolete. Her aunts in Scotland, who had prospered by the investment of a thousand pounds in South Australia, generously made up the lost income afterwards. Mention of all these monetary details is not irrelevant to any record of Catherine Spence's early days: she gives them full importance in her own memoirs, as she was obliged to do in her life, and the calculation and balancing of small but never trivial sums of money perpetually claimed her attention. Later, turning this discipline to account, as she turned every other, she could be of more practical use on destitute boards and hospital committees than men and women who thought of money only in careless or ignorant approximations.

Meanwhile she grew wealthy in the number and quality of her friends and in intellectual associations. This sufficed. She never knew the intimate love of any man, but she was artist enough to deplore this only because a love affair – 'even disappointed love', she says – might have benefited certain aspects of her work; it might also have distracted her in certain other aspects.

In 1859 she read John Stuart Mill's advocacy of Hare's system of proportional representation, and after that, she declares, the reform of the electoral system became the foremost object of her life. Already a novelist, a poet and a journalist, she became also a pamphleteer. The thought of service to humanity was now to lie behind all her writings. Her third novel, *Mr Hogarth's Will*, built on a theme of feminist propaganda, contained also an exposition of effective voting, and chiefly for this reason the Melbourne *Telegraph* bought the serial rights for fifty pounds. When this book was published in England, it was over her full name, now being used in print for the first time. Thereafter that name came to be recognized more widely with every year that passed.

After the completion of this book the bounty of two friends

enabled her to visit England and Scotland and the Continent; and there she met and exchanged ideas with some notable men and women, including John Stuart Mill, Thomas Hare, Rowland Hill and George Eliot.

After her return to Australia her activities continued to multiply and her interests to widen. Upon the completion of her fourth novel, *The Author's Daughter*, she began the study of Latin with a schoolboy nephew, and presently she embarked upon her lecturing career. This was another pioneering venture for a woman. For the rest of her long life she lectured both here and in America on literary subjects and public questions. The Unitarian Church had meantime become the church – as Australia had become the country – of her adoption, and from its pulpit she preached more than a hundred original sermons. Her public work increased: she was the first woman appointed to the Board of Advice under the Education Department in South Australia; she did splendid practical pioneering work for state children; she gave her help to the woman's suffrage movement; she was a foundation member of the South Australian Hospital Commission; at the age of sixty-eight she made a worldwide lecture tour; and still she carried her banner with the device of proportional representation. She wrote one or two more novels, but these brought her little return, and she seems to have taken this failure of her more ambitious literary career with a rather surprising philosophy: with all her splendid capacity for logic, and all her fine sense of equity, Catherine Helen Spence meekly, and even deprecatingly, accepted the fact that one might put months of one's life into the construction of a book, know it to be well reviewed, widely read and appreciated by the public and be paid for it with a coolie's wage and six printed copies of the work.

When she was eighty-four years of age she undertook the writing of her autobiography, but it was left for friends and relatives to finish. At the time of her death she was still engaged in literary work, still ardently pursuing her social reforms, and widely known as Australia's grand old woman. Catherine Helen Spence was one who took her share of the colonial self-consciousness and sublimated it.

*II*

The name of Ada Cambridge falls naturally into place after that of Catherine Spence. She, too, was transplanted from the old world, but at an age and from an environment that influenced her outlook on the new country somewhat differently. She was born in 1844, at Wigginhall, St Germains, Norfolk, a very address that seems to smack of the English conservatism of her class; a conservatism which, for all the countering warmth of her temperament, and all the humanitarian comprehension of her sympathies, remained in her to the last.

In 1870 she married the Rev. G. F. Cross, who was already committed to his ministry in Australia when she met him, and they sailed together a month after the wedding. Even at that comparatively late day, reliable information about the colonies was hard to obtain, and people offering it appeared to have little idea of proportion, either in a geographical sense or any other. Knowing that they were to come to Victoria, one friend encouraged them with a most urbane picture of episcopal life in Melbourne; but Melbourne, for the time being at least, was not their destination. Theirs was to be a bush parish, and in her reminiscent *Thirty Years in Australia* Ada Cambridge says that she then thought of the bush as 'a vast shrubbery with occasional spears hurtling through it'. This short, decriptive phrase not only gives rather more than a hint of the writer's humour, but the picture of an English shrubbery assailed by outlandish weapons is peculiarly significant here: for the English shrubbery might be taken as the mental heritage of the writer, and we can imagine life in Australia making many a startling assault upon it.

Ada Cambridge grew to love and to admire the land of her adoption, but she never became completely knit with it in the way Catherine Spence did. For the rest of her life, being in Australia, she was yet not altogether of it. Her books of the country dealt with times and realities a little removed from those of her own experience, as if, while she shirked nothing that came in the way of living contacts, her imagination kept its freedom in surveying things at a little distance. She, too, had all the desires of the social reformer, but she was of a delicate physical constitution, and emotional, and consequently was more capable of the essential indignation than of the constructive patience equally needed to accomplish broad social changes. Besides, she had been born into that order of 'closed' morality from which positive reformers seldom come.

She was gallant, adventurous, and extremely versatile, and life for her was a vital existence. It was long before she was to come to rest among the clerical urbanities of Melbourne. That initial bush parish of the envisioned spears turned out to be the first of seven such. The literal spears may have been missing, but there were plenty of other excitements, and dangers more than occasional, and deaths even among her children just as sudden-dealt. From place to place she went with her husband, through a long succession of years, setting up rectories in the wilderness and dispensing from them every imaginable human service. If she ever made any of the time-honoured protests of the parson's wife, about having married the man and not the parish, it was only as a matter of principle and in defence of her feminine kind.

She wrote, in all, twenty-eight novels and a fair amount of poetry and miscellaneous other work, but she never came to regard herself as a professional writer. 'Housework,' she says, 'has all along been the business of life; novels have been squeezed into the odd times.' And, speaking of her first Australian home: 'We papered the back part (of the house) ourselves. I made the drugget and matting floor-coverings, the chintz curtains, the dimity bed-furniture – made everything, in fact, that was sewable . . . When I remember the time-honoured theory that a writing person is no good for anything else, I feel obliged, at the risk of appearing a braggart, to parade the above fact.' In 1873 her journal records: 'G. and I making a dining-table,' and 'G. and I making a sideboard.' Sometimes it seems that Fanny Trollope's tragic and astounding exemplification of a woman's ability to superimpose authorship on an already overfull burden of other tasks became a curse upon women writers following her. Ada Cambridge, to have produced all she did amid such crowding interests, must have been blessed with a talent quick and obedient.

She had begun to write at an early age, and more or less in secret, and her first published work was a hymn for a church magazine. This was followed by other hymns, which were presently collected in a small volume; and she then started to write short stories for religious magazines, and some verse. These early poems were the forerunners of others really notable. The poetry she produced later, at different periods throughout her life, reveals an altogether dissimilar outlook to that of her prose writings. This is quite usual in the work of almost any writer who has written both poetry and prose, but in Ada Cambridge it is singularly marked. Some of the poems of her middle life are positively radical in thought, and coming upon them for the first time after some other previous acquaintance with the writer one might experience a little shock of surprise. Could this have been the young lady from Wigginhall? But every radical is a sentimentalist underneath, and, remembering that, it is not so hard to see the mental causeway upon which Ada Cambridge might cross quite easily from one sociological extreme to another, and back again, for she never burnt her bridges. Her collected poems were published as late as 1913, and there is a further peculiar interest in this, that the volume contained a number that had originally been published many years before and withdrawn. These republished poems are remarkable for their vigour and frankness; but at the same time they were first produced escaping individualism was apt to be summarily caught and re-confined; even its author might subsequently come to feel that it was not expedient for it to remain at large; so Ada Cambridge's first mature poems were withdrawn immediately after their earlier publication, and the author was sixty-nine years of age when they were again brought out.

Shortly after her arrival in Australia she began contributing to the *Australasian* and the *Argus*. She wrote with shrewdness and humour and employed a fresher and sharper idiom than was then common. *Up the Murray*, published as a serial in 1875, not only brought her welcome payment in money (this was in the happy days before syndicated journalism), but also attracted the attention of an intellectual circle among the wealthy and established 'squatting' families of Victoria. Certain of these families opened their doors to her with that superb colonial hospitality that marked the era; and from the multifarious demands of husband and babies, choir members and district visitors, sick parishioners and immigrant servants, stranded travellers and new chums with or without letters of introduction, she found a refuge with congenial minds in the dignified niceties and compensating freedoms of a society to which she was herself most adapted. This was the society that encouraged her to write, and it would be largely through the eyes of this society she would see her own fictional characters and incidents; perhaps that is one reason she never approached these characters and incidents too nearly. Her novels are romantic, but not sentimental or subjective; if Ada

Cambridge was a sentimentalist she was too subtle a one to display it in this manner. Her heroines are generally of a splendidly active physique, more common-sensible than sensitive, and with what one might call a fine colonial flavour; and their stories are sane and pleasant stories.

She wrote the autobiographical *Thirty Years in Australia* when she was approaching her sixtieth year; it was the first and more important of two books of reminiscences. And as it belongs among those simple records of life that have a more durable quality than fiction, it can still be read with real interest.

The colonial self-consciousness showed itself through Ada Cambridge characteristically in a wariness towards all mass developments, social and political, in the new country; she had a fine apprehension, not only of the movements of her own day, but of their outcome in subsequent movements. And she showed herself happiest in the contemplation of those kindred Australian growths that still retained the essential elements of their English origin. Only when she paid a visit to England in her latter years did she realize how far from her birthplace she herself had actually grown.

## III

Our first native-born writer of any importance was Mrs Campbell Praed, but little of her adult life was spent in Australia. Born Rosa Caroline Murray Prior, she belonged to a well-known station family in southern Queensland, and her life and writings do not depart from the traditions of this family, for its members, still maintaining their primary interest in the land, had a flair for gentility and did not lack sophistication; one had left some reputation as an amateur poet, and Rosa Caroline's father had important political and official connections in the colony throughout the greatest part of his life.

The writer herself was born in 1851, on the Logan River, and she spent her observant childhood in the bush, amid surroundings of natural beauty and even grandeur. Bush life then, in easy circumstances, was a life of peculiar satisfaction for a child, but it became an existence of ennui for the unoccupied young woman later, and Mrs Campbell Praed has revealed this in the character of many of her heroines and in the tone of a number of her books. She attended school in Brisbane, where she saw something of local society and politics, and then she returned home to invent amusement for herself and any other young people of the district. During these days she edited the *Marroon Magazine*, a local MS production, to which she vainly tried to persuade Brunton Stephens, then a tutor on a nearby station, to contribute his afterwards celebrated *Convict Once*. She read such books of the day as could be procured, and when the supply of ready-made romance ran low she made up the deficiency in her own willing imagination.

When she was twenty-one she married Campbell Praed, son of a London banker and nephew of the poet Winthrop Mackworth Praed. They went to live on Curtis Island, off the Queensland coast, where they went in for cattle-raising, then the staple industry of the colony. They remained on the island for nearly four years, and she afterwards wrote of their experiences in *The Romance of a Station*. Life there, after the first novelty had worn off, must have been monotonous enough, but she could at least recognize the practical advantage of an island in that no one could brand their calves and the cattle could not stray away. They sold the island ultimately, however, and went to England and remained there.

Not until 1880, when she was settled in London, did Mrs Campbell Praed begin writing seriously, so in one sense it may be straining a point to call her an Australian writer. But she made up for her defection by writing most assiduously, for many years after, of the country she had left, and in doing this she tried to present a sincere and interesting picture of Australia, and, in her own words, 'to aid in bridging over the gulf which divides the old world from the young'.

Her first book was *An Australian Heroine*, and its acceptance was advised by George Meredith, who was then the publisher's reader. This book has its first scene laid on Curtis Island, but its heroine, living there under the most extraordinary circumstances and a creature of her strange environment, can hardly be called typically Australian. Mrs Praed's heroines are sufficiently varied in their physical characteristics and the circumstances of their lives, but they are all one in their romantic imaginations and proclivities. She wrote exclusively, too, from the feminine viewpoint; male characters almost invariably seem to be introduced only for the sake of, and entirely as affecting, the heroine. And these heroines are mostly young women of the

1870s, and their stories are chronicles of sentiment. Theirs was, after all, a sentimental generation. But Mrs Praed went on writing almost up to the time of her death in 1935, and in respect of Australia her outlook never became modernized; in the period of the country's fastest growth she had no cognisance, or made no recognition, of it, and she continued to draw her Australian heroines with the attributes of the 1870s. In spite of their emotional yearnings, however, these young women were of a normally healthy, outdoor type; one feels that they knew the freedom of the open heavens even if they were rather addicted to star-gazing. The consciousness of the elements, of physical space and freshness, and of new fields for endeavour is in Mrs Praed's depiction of bush life and pioneering; and then it is interesting and amusing to find, worked into her colourful colonial scene, a distinct pattern of English etiquette and social usage, threads, as it were, of Mrs Gaskell's proprieties woven into the newer convention.

In all, she wrote about thirty novels, three of them in collaboration with Justin McCarthy, another romantic after her own heart. About half of her books have an Australian theme or Australian characters, and they were once best sellers in England and America. Her work is not the less readable or admirable because, beyond the simple picturing of an Australian colony, she had no propagandist's axe to grind. Also, when she comes to describe or comment upon any matter or question of historic importance, she does so with a remarkable fairness and balance of judgement; one has an instance of this in her observations upon the extremely vexed problem of the Aborigine in the days of settlement, a problem that usually meets with squeamish or callous indifference, on the one hand, or a lop-sided sentimentality on the other.

Mrs Praed is remembered among those who knew her personally as a woman of beauty and charm, and one whose ways lay in pleasant places. Here was a woman writer on whom the curse of Fanny Trollope did not fall. One cannot imagine her writing with the aid of a night-light on one corner of a table littered with medicine bottles and socks waiting to be darned; her house in London was gracious and beautiful, and we hear of her entertaining distinguished company in a 'lemon yellow drawing room and a sealing wax red dining room hung with native weapons and spears and bits of tappa' – momentoes of the antipodes preserved in Norfolk Square.

*IV*

It is a delightful privilege to strain a point again and claim Mme Couvreur as another pioneer Australian woman writer in spite of her Dutch-French parentage, English birth, Belgian marriage, and long Continental residence and professional career. She has been called, by people who cannot get away from systems of category and comparison, 'the Australian Jane Austen' and 'the Australian George Eliot', but without bringing her under the patents of any other writer's name we may remember her simply as the 'Tasma' of her own titling, and Australian enough by such an implication.

She was, in the beginning, Jessie Catherin Huybers, born in Highgate, London, in October 1848. Her father came of a long line of Dutch merchants and mariners. In 1852 he brought his family out on the long voyage to Hobart Town, and there he established a large warehouse business. His family grew as this business prospered; Jessie Catherin was the second child and eldest daughter of seven, so that her early imaginativeness was not the reaction of solitude but a gift happily developed for the entertainment of younger children.

There was ample scope for her imagination, and material for it to work upon. Beyond the pleasant territory of her home, under the shadow of Mt Wellington and overlooking one of the loveliest natural bays in the world, the crudely built capital of the Tasmanian colony offended her childish eye, so it was airily obliterated, and her fancy built there a new and splendid city, the architectural delights of which must have beggared any description but her own. The surrounding bush, beautiful in itself, was acceptable as it existed, with the excitement of a real bushranger now and then, or the melancholy apparition of a passing convict gang always taken into account.

Throughout her life and writings the elements of human sorrow, maladjustments and difficulty were never obliterated, like the merely material ugliness of bad town-planning, from the world that Tasma recognized; seeing their inevitability very early, if only objectively then, she came to assimilate them with the wholesome and pleasant parts of life, not stupidly, but with a truly sensitive philosophy.

She made her first appearance in print at the age of sixteen with some highly tragic verses entitled, 'Lines Addressed by a Mother to Her Idiot Son'. Her choice may have fallen upon such a theme by some outward prompting or by her own errant fancy; certainly had she possessed intuition or the capacity for handling it, she would have shown herself already a greater genius than she ever actually was.

Some years elapsed before she took up a literary career in earnest. In 1867, when she was nineteen, she married a man whose very name surviving members of her family now wish to be forgotten; he was a racing man and a member of a Victorian station family. It was a most unhappy venture, and, after living with him for a little time in Melbourne, she separated from him and subsequently obtained a divorce.

Her mother took her to London in 1873, and it was upon her return to Australia that she took the pseudonym of 'Tasma' and began contributing to the *Australasian* and the *Melbourne Review*. Her first short story, 'Barren Love', appeared in 1878 and was afterwards included in a volume of stories published under the title of *A Sydney Sovereign*.

Again she went abroad, this time to make her permanent home in Europe, and there, like Catherine Spence, she came to divide her time between lecturing and writing. The fine cultural education she had received in her youth, largely from her partly French mother, enabled her to enter into French journalism under a standard far more exacting than any she had known in Australia. An article in the *Nouvelle Revue*, advocating European emigration to the Tasmanian fruit-growing areas, attracted the attention of the Geographical Society of Paris, and she was invited to speak on the subject; this initial address was repeated in Holland and Belgium, and her lecturing career had begun. Throughout this career she never faced an audience without suffering the most painful nervousness, but always, after the first few minutes, her old childish pleasure in amusing and informing others came to her rescue, and during that period, when the public lecture was about the most popular form of intellectual entertainment in Europe, she won much acclaim. Halls were crowded whenever she spoke. The French government conferred upon her the title of *Officer de l'Academie* with silver palms; she was presented with medals in the French provinces, and the king of the Belgians received her in private audience to discuss schemes for improving the means of communication between Belgium and Australia. What an anodyne, all this, for past disillusioning experiences in Victoria!

But when she came to writing her first novel she remembered Australia and produced *Uncle Piper of Piper's Hill*, one of the best of the early Australian novels. In saying here that she 'remembered Australia', one does not forget all those previous references to the country she had left; she had written and lectured on Australian subjects often enough before, but there is an intimacy between fiction and its author that does not enter into the other more formal relationship. *Uncle Piper* was published in 1888. By this time the Australian period of her life was ended; she had grown out of its childhood; its later episodes were closed; her Australian marriage had been dissolved: now her home was in Brussels; her contacts were European; she had been for three years married to M. Auguste Couvreur, Belgian intellectual and statesman; she spoke and customarily wrote the language of her husband and of ancestors who had not known Australia, yet it was of everything Australian that she came to construct her first novel. The colonial 'consciousness' had followed her across the world. Of course she need not have given it indulgence, but the fact that she did is proof also of that assimilatory power we have before noticed, her wise sense of the integration of life. It is not surprising that Mrs Campbell Praed, settled in London, should have written 'Australian' books there, but it is remarkable that Mme Couvreur wrote *Uncle Piper of Piper's Hill* in a salon in Brussels.

Even if it had not been a very good book, nice feeling must have prompted us to acknowledge it, and, though it has now faded into some dim corner of the last century, it was a good book. Several others followed, but did not come up to the interest of the first. Tasma died in 1897 while she was yet comparatively young. Any speculation upon her longer life brings with it a speculation upon the co-existent life of her Australian 'self-consciousness', but there is proof that that feeling, under conditions that did not foster it, still lasted well.

## V

When we come now to the memory of Louisa Atkinson, it appears like a miniature in a portrait gallery. 'One of the most interesting of Australia's daughters', Dr Woolls called her, and Australia can claim her more fully than any other woman writer of her day.

Caroline Louisa Waring Atkinson, to give her the full name that must have been rather overwhelming for such a dryad-like creature, was born, in 1834, at Oldbury on the southern highlands of New South Wales. The estate, with its dignified stone homestead embowered in English trees, was part of a large grant made to her father, James Atkinson, a government official, in 1822. Her father died a few weeks after her birth, and her mother subsequently married again. This second marriage of her mother's seemed to make little difference in the life of Louisa, as she was familiarly called, and it never affected their close association. She was a delicate child and Mrs Atkinson, or Mrs Barton, as she subsequently became, undertook her education at home. This was fortunate enough in itself, for her teacher was a woman of unusual culture and attainments, and Louisa's tuition in writing, drawing, languages and natural history was particularly suited to her natural talents. Later she took up the study of botany, zoology and geology, all of which were applicable to the work she undertook when she became old enough.

The countryside about Berrima and Sutton Forest provided ample opportunity for fieldwork in these sciences at first. Except for the few estates like Oldbury, which had been partly cleared and planted with English gardens, the land was virgin and unspoiled, with the huge mounds of the termites' nests among the eucalyptus trees and the platypus still in hiding under the riverbanks. Leaving Oldbury, she lived for a little time with her mother at Burwood, then an outer suburb very sparsely settled. But her health still giving cause for anxiety, her mother presently bought land at Kurrajong Heights and built the house there known as Fernhurst until its demolition years ago. This district, sloping picturesquely down to the Hawkesbury, became Louisa's hunting ground.

There she became a still more serious student of botany and natural history; she began to publish her observations and attracted the attention of established and authoritative Australian scientists by her work. If she also attracted the scandalized notice of local inhabitants as she explored the hills and gullies of the Upper Hawkesbury, clad in the unorthodox but convenient costume she adopted for her excursions, they too came to accept her at last and to know her with affection. But she must have seemed strangely exotic to these people in the beginning; she remained delicate in health, but all her slender strength was charged with her enthusiasm; she was dark-eyed and gentle and swift-moving; her proper place might have seemed always with the birds and the trees and the small bush animals. But they came to discover in her a capable and understanding charity; she became the unpaid scribe of the district, where many people were unlettered and depended on her to do any necessary writing for them, even to drawing up their wills; the old and the sick trusted in her capacity to help them; she was the confidante of children and organized and taught the first Sunday school in the district – and one cannot help thinking that the vocation of Sunday-school teaching must have lost nothing by the application of a competent botanist.

By this time she had become a very competent botanist indeed; so competent that Baron von Mueller used much of the data she collected in his afterwards world-famous compilations, naming several native botanical species after her. She, meanwhile, was writing popular scientific and nature study articles for publication in Sydney papers, some of which were later re-published overseas. The *Sydney Mail* regularly printed work almost from the date of its inception; for this paper and the *Sydney Morning Herald* she wrote a long series of sketches under the title 'A Voice from the Country', and similar articles appeared in the *Horticultural Magazine* in the early 1860s. She also wrote many articles generally descriptive of the Hawkesbury district and prepared a botanical survey of the Hawkesbury.

When she was twenty-three years of age, her first book was published in Sydney. Her ambition had not run to a two-volume novel, and this was an unpretentious story called *Gertrude, the Immigrant Girl*. A year or two later it was followed by *Cowanda*, and several stories after were published serially in the *Herald* and were very popular.

Having returned to Oldbury, in 1870 she married James Calvert Snowdon, another amateur botanist of some distinction. Some years older than herself, he had come to Australia on the ship with Leichhardt and had accompanied the explorer on his hazardous expedition to Port Essington in 1844–5.

Louisa's last story was published serially in 1872. In that year she died suddenly, leaving an infant daughter.

These are five unforgotten Australian women. Now they live on in our memories, supposedly because of the things that they once wrote; but, in the words of Jacques Chevalier, 'That which truly matters in a man's work, gives it meaning, is its life and the part of it which will endure, is not so much what he said as what he meant to say'; let us be mindful of this in thinking of them.

It has always seemed to the writer that even the most inconsiderable biography should not be completed without a humble apology for those misconstructions and misinterpretations that have been inadvertently put into it, and I would make that apology now to the several subjects of this memorial.

# MARGARET PRESTON

## Pioneer Women Artists

The Oxford Dictionary defines 'pioneer' as 'one of a body of foot soldiers marching in advance with spades, etc., to prepare the road for the main body'. The world has been much enlarged, but there is still in it that kernel of hard primitive effort. This is not irresponsible adventuring but adventuring with spades; the pioneer is the leader who does more than lead, who makes a way for others to follow. In Australia the way of the pioneer artist was as difficult as the way of the pioneer farmer, his field, or her field, as virgin and as pathless as the wilderness. For in Australia there is no traditional basis of art. There is no folklore art to be the link between the individual artist and the soil. The artist started at scratch, with mind and hand oriented to a different world. He had to discover Australia before he could give back its image in his work, a discovery in which the first clue, the folk stage, is forever missing and irreplaceable. However art is conceived, as cosmopolitan, or as an intensely national and local function, as I conceive it, Australia has offered great difficulties to the pioneer artist. Its strangeness (how could it be 'in the blood' of those first artists here?), its isolation from art centres and their stimulation, the lack of art schools, were all handicaps. It is, however, a law of nature that wherever a community is planted there will grow up in its midst, no matter with what difficulty, an art to express it. Today there are many Australian artists, famous abroad and at home, who have sought out the earth's secret and brought to Australia the cosmopolitan art of the world. Women have had their part in this from the beginning.

The first of whom there is a record is Jane Elizabeth Currie. Her husband, Captain Currie, came to Australia with Captain Stirling, who founded the colony of Western Australia. Mrs Currie seems to have felt the excitement of the new and strange land for all the work that remains is a record of the new scene. There is a sketch, 'Our First Hut on Garden Island', dated June 1829, and a view of Cockburn Sound, showing HMS *Challenger* and the sloop *Sulphur* at anchor, done at the same time. With her panorama of the Swan River, ten feet by one foot, she *still* holds the Australian record for size. She left also many studies of wildflowers and an illustrated diary covering the period July 1829 to August 1832. A specimen of her work can be seen in Sydney, where an enlargement of her miniature of her husband hangs in the Pioneers' Club.

The first woman artist to be born in Australia was Adelaide Ironside. She was born in Sydney in 1831 and grew up quietly in her home at Crow's Nest, North Sydney, painting, writing poetry and studying languages with her mother, an accomplished and highly educated woman. She was a delicate girl, the only surviving child of her parents, and seems to have early attracted attention by her brilliance. Dr Lang, who had baptized her at Scots' Church, was her life-long friend, and she won the admiration of Sir Charles Nicholson and Daniel Henry Daniehy for her gifts. It was decided that she must study abroad. In 1855, when she was twenty-four, her mother took her to London, where she met Ruskin, who wrote her many letters, imbuing her with his philosophy of the good, the true, the beautiful, and giving her philosophical, or, you might say, metaphysical, lessons in the drawing of a shell. She went to Rome to study. Everything was made easy for the brilliant girl. The Pope gave her an audience which resulted in permission to copy pictures in the Vatican and leave to study fresco painting under a monk in Perugia. At first she appears to have had money difficulties, and Dr Lang proposed a motion in the New South Wales parliament that she should be granted two hundred pounds a year to enable her to continue her studies. This, and help from friends, she proudly refused. Soon there was no need of help. She was selling her pictures. The Prince of Wales bought one for five hundred pounds, W. C. Wentworth another for a similar sum. In 1862 she exhibited two pictures in the New South Wales court of the London Exhibition. The pictures were 'The Marriage in Cana of Galilee', a canvas that showed the strong influence on her work of the Italian masters, and a more original self-portrait, 'The Pilgrim of Art'. Here she is kneeling at the feet of her mother, who crowns her with a laurel wreath. At the corner of the picture she has printed, *'Ars Longa*

*Vita Brevis.*' Our pioneer artist evidently knew her own worth and had the quality of not minding who knew it.

Many famous men came to her studio, and her early death, aged thirty-six at the Palazzo Albani, in Rome, on 15 April 1867, after two years of illness, was a deep sorrow to her friends. One of them, writing her obituary in the *Athenæm*, said of her: 'Full of nervous sensibility, she was the impersonation of Genius, her mind was too active for the delicate frame in which it dwelt and it did not require the gift of Prophecy to see that one possessed of so many endowments would soon pass away.'

Francis Adams praised her pictures highly for their quiet feeling and their deep but muted passion, but it seems a pity that her native land did not benefit more from her great talents. This country needs its artists, writers and poetesses, and when they settle in foreign lands they are betraying the land of their birth.

When three of Adelaide Ironside's finest pictures were brought to Australia after her death they received scant courtesy. The pictures were 'The Pilgrim of Art', 'The Marriage in Cana of Galilee' and 'The Presentation of the Magi to the Infant Jesus'. They were lent to the National Art Gallery, then housed in a temporary building, almost a shed, and here they exposed to wind and dust and were badly damaged, particularly 'The Pilgrim of Art'. They are, for all their interest and the ability they show, a poor remnant of the woman whose life promised so much and of whom Brunton Stephens could write: 'O love, O mine, and thy seemingly broken endeavour/Here re-appeareth, transfigured as thou; yet the art of thy youth/And the light of the spirit of beauty is on it for ever and ever, For art is the garment of praise, and the broidered apparel of truth.'

There are other women who did their pioneering nearer home and who must be mentioned in this record, however briefly. There are three who did much by their flower and plant studies to arouse interest in our native flora. They were Caroline Waring Atkinson, Louisa Meredith and Maria Ellis Rowan.

Caroline Atkinson was an excellent botanical artist, inheriting the gift from her mother. She was a writer as well as an artist, and an account of her life and her literary work appears in the article on pioneer women writers. She contributed many articles with illustrations to various magazines, on native plants, their uses among the Aborigines and their possibilities. These are scattered, and there is a good work for someone to do in collecting these records and drawings and making them available to students. Our native plants gradually become extinct where civilization pushes out, bringing other flowers and other animals from overseas and so making a complete change in our flora and fauna. Caroline Atkinson died in 1872 and her obituary pays tribute to her work for its 'unaffected elegance and extreme accuracy'.

Louisa Meredith was not Australian by birth but came here with her husband in 1839. Like Adelaide Ironside and Caroline Atkinson, her gifts came from and were fostered by an accomplished mother and, like Jane Currie, she responded eagerly to her new environment. At twenty-one she had published a book of original poems and drawings that had attracted much interest. After her arrival in Australia, all her artistic energies were concentrated on the new country and its beauties. In the intervals of running a home and rearing a family she produced ten books, most illustrated by herself. Among them was *Some of My Bush Friends in Tasmania, Native Flowers and Some Insects and Berries* (1866), a book fourteen-and-a-half by ten inches, containing about a dozen full-plate coloured illustrations and many fine, dainty drawings with bright descriptions by the artist. She also wrote and illustrated a book on the fishes of the east coast and has left a record of a trip to the Victorian goldfields in 1856. Her books were published in England and had a wide sale, helping considerably to make Australian flowers and scenes known overseas. She was painting till within a year of her death in 1895.

Maria Ellis Rowan was a native of Melbourne, born there in 1848. She married Captain Rowan, a hero of the Maori wars, and spent most of her life travelling and recording in paint the wildflowers wherever she went – in New Zealand, New Guinea, Queensland, Western Australia. She spent twelve years in America and, with Miss B. Lounsbury, published a three-volume work on American flora. Her output was enormous. There are nine hundred and forty-seven paintings by her in the National Library in Canberra alone, one hundred and twenty-five in the Queensland Museum in Brisbane and examples in all the national galleries of Australia. Her work was very popular during her lifetime and to discuss her medals would be a task in arithmetic. Her death occurred in 1922.

To pass to other fields, there are some lithographs, dated 1836 – at one time in the possession of the late Miss Rose

Scott – by Maria Barney, daughter of Colonel Barney, sometime Surveyor-general of the colony, and a pupil of Conrad Martens. Melbourne may claim Mrs Alexander Murison McCrae, who arrived there in 1841, as one of her pioneer women artists. During a busy life – of which we have a partial record in her diary, edited by her grandson Hugh McCrae, she sketched the landscapes and flowers of her adopted land and executed a number of beautiful miniatures, including a self-portrait, in which she is wearing the McCrae tartan. Most of her work is in the possession of the family. Her death occurred in 1934.

A pioneer portrait painter was Catherine Elizabeth Streeter. Born in Ireland in 1842, she arrived in Melbourne in the 1850s. She became a teacher in the Victorian Education Department. Her picture 'Manfred', inspired by a scene in Byron's poem, gained for her a *Mention Honorable* at the 1879 Exhibition at Paris. She held a show of her work in Brisbane when she was eighty-one and died in January 1930, leaving an autobiography dating back to the 1850s. Her principal portraits are of Dean Hayes, of Saint Augustine's Orphanage, Geelong, the Rev. William Quick, Queen's College, University of Melbourne, and Margary Collard Smith.

There was also that wonderful Margaret Baskerville, who was the first women in Australia to complete a statue, that of Sir Thomas Bent. It is enormous, standing on a pedestal twelve feet high. Her death occurred in 1930.

Theo Cowan was the first woman born in Sydney to take sculpture as a profession. Ethel Stephens, also born in Sydney, was president of the Women Painters' Society for years, and Thea Proctor was president of the contemporary group, born at Armidale, New South Wales. With these last three artists we arrive at 1938, still pioneers in art. And yet the spade had not dug deep enough. The Australian school still remains to be founded. There must not be any pleasure trips of scuttling to the Antipodes for help; the pioneers must develop themselves from groups of artists who all have the one idea of Australian forms, etc. A voice crying in the wilderness is of no use; this only makes individualism, not nationalism. The days of the pioneer in art are still with us, albeit with more comfort, but also with more temptations. We have yet to prepare the road for the main body.

(Acknowledgment is made to William Moore's *Story of Australian Art* for much of the information in this article, and to Miss Margaret Swann for information concerning Caroline Atkinson and Louisa Meredith. MP)

# KATHLEEN MONYPENNY

## Snow in London

The white snow falls softly,
fluttering downwards like small delicate birds,
      brushing the trees
  embroidered in fine black
    against the wintry sky.
   As I watch them
     my heart is happy without thought.
Though the snow comes quickly,
  blown through the palpable air,
    I remember a red rose
  branching against the sea's warm blue.
Tho' the skies are grey and the wind howls,
  the slender bare trees are silver in the gloom,
and I remember moonlight on the yellow cassia hedge,
    the scent of an incense plant
     in the warm night,
    the colour of flowers and grass
     beneath a summer moon.
Altho' I cannot forget them,
  my heart is happy and at peace;
I can put out my hand
  and *touch* them still;
Distance and Time dissolved.
Far away can be very near
  and the near so very far away,
    while Now the precious
     or terrible moment
     falls past like the snow,
    like the wind.

# Kylie Tennant

## Pioneering Still Goes On

There are people who give a little jerk of distaste politely controlled if you mention the word 'pioneer'. They flinch from it as others do from jazz, as from something blatant. To many it is a word associated with obituaries in suburban newspapers, with politicians, after-dinner eloquence, and the self-consciousness of a young country over-eager to force a tradition to grow under glass instead of waiting for a slow maturation.

Any small settler who has injudiciously picked a bad spot in a high range and lived there in defiance of probability is likely to squeeze into the pioneer class. The more sceptical of us still have our doubts whether some of the earlier settlers were pioneers in any true sense. We doubt whether they had done anything really extraordinary in making for a new land. Thousands had done just what they did, going somewhere where they thought they would be better off than at home.

Australians are so close to the first settlers that they know too much about them and are inclined to feel rather the irritation aroused by relatives than the veneration due to ancestors between whom and their descendants the broad plains of tradition have spread a lush peaceable distance.

Then, again, we must lay to Henry Lawson the affectionate charge of linking in our minds the idea of women pioneers with outback settlers' wives. In any number of stories, simple, lovable, pathetic, he hammered out the type of the bush woman, her strength, independence and patience, until, if you say 'pioneer', the vague response is likely to be, 'Oh, yes, I know, "Women of the West" and all that sort of thing. My grandmother was one. Had thirteen children and worked like a slave. Marvellous old girl.' This example of superb logic is a deduction based on the premise that all early settlers were pioneers; if they were not, why were they early settlers?

Pioneering, however, is not confined to a colonial environment. It is a matter firstly of character and secondly of opportunity. A pioneer may be defined as a person who surveys his environment, decides it isn't good enough, sees what is needed, and gets to work to supply the need. This takes a number of complex qualities, ranging from independence, vision, concentration and selflessness to a ruthless disregard for other people's corns. So much for character; now for opportunity. I maintain the finest pioneer work being done in Australia today is in the capital cities because the cities are offering opportunities for it that the countryside does not.

Everywhere in the cities there is a mushroom growth of small societies, of groups of enthusiasts, heaving up the flagstones of tradition. There are hundreds of organizations, small and large, wearing out political doormats, presenting petitions, writing letters to the newspspers, calling attention to the state of slums, prisons, schools, roads, taxes, the unemployed, the maternal death-rate, asylums, hospitals, the status of women, free speech, libraries, child welfare, censorship, baby clinics, kindergartens, parks and playgrounds, physical education, opera or parliamentary expenditure. They are doing their best to improve, not only their own environment, but everyone else's. They are vociferous, assiduous, often jealous of each other, and a pest to those in high places. They get themselves publicity in the newspapers. They cry aloud and sometimes their voice is heard and they get things done.

Hacking away in the undergrowth of resolutions, conferences, deputations and debates, you are most likely to find the lineal descendants of those tough settlers who first decided that the standards of Australia's early black inhabitants were not good enough for them. In the heart of each organization you will discover some kind of honorary secretary, the enthusiast, not infrequently a woman, who started the thing and has done most of the work.

There is an interesting aspect of modern pioneering that goes almost unnoticed. It is the organization, by a polite fiction, not a group of individuals, which beards ministers in their dens and demands improvements to our social structure. Pioneers have accreted organizations much in the way shell-fish do a shell for the purposes of protection and stability. They realize that, just as gold-mining passed from the individual diggers to great companies with modern machinery, so social reconstruction can no longer be brought about by individual action but requires the backing of an organization.

The complex working of city life demands co-operation. Take an excellent example in the playground beside the approach to the Sydney Harbour Bridge. It was a public-spirited alderman of the City Council who suggested that the playground be built. The council fitted the playground with most of the latest and best facilities for sport and athletics; but just as important as the playground are the trained supervisors supplied by the Board of Social Studies. Without them the playground might easily degenerate into an anarchy run by the bullies. With them it has become a valuable means for the cultural and physical well-being of over a thousand children.

It is true that this organizational type of pioneering is not now confined to the cities; we may point, for example, to the nurses of the Australian Inland Mission. To them belongs the credit of appreciably raising the standard of living in many an outback settlement. Often their hospitals are the only centre of social life and civilization for many miles of scrub and plain. They have been instrumental in having men's clubs set up, in sending to lonely places books, magazines, and sometimes even flowers, all of them more wistfully desired than coast-dwellers may imagine. The Inland Mission's headquarters have enabled the women of the Never-Never to operate transceiver sets, whereby they may talk through a hundred miles of air as through a crack in the back fence. But these nurses are one illustration of my point that pioneering has passed into a new stage, where it is most characterized by brilliant organizing. Without the support of groups of women and women's organizations to back the vision of 'Flynn of the Inland', it is almost certain that there would have been no nurses, no flying medical service, no radio receiving and transmitting sets in lonely homesteads.

The upholder of individual effort is about to interrupt. He points to a 'pioneer' settler on the Queensland border or in Central Australia who started with a patch of prickly pear and now puts into practice all the newest methods of water conservation, sheep and cattle raising, whose wife has a fine house with electric light, hot-water jug, cleaner, fans, patent cooler, radio, and most of the comforts of the city. Again, this is a matter of character and opportunity. One might, in reply, point to the paradox of families living within six miles of the Sydney General Post Office in bag and tin huts, a man, woman and children, all huddled in the one miserable shelter, half starved and never properly clothed. The superhuman effort by which the wives of some men on the dole keep themselves and their children decent would make the exploits of the big station owner pale by comparison. Their bravery, owing to the circumstances in which it is exercised, is never as apparent as a colourful financial success.

Admittedly, outback Australia provides, of all places in the world, the opportunity for pioneers. We are one of the few nations that still possess an expanding frontier and with that frontier such problems as isolation, the displacement of a native race, difficulties of transport, lack of educational and medical facilities. There are still two million square miles with less than one person to the square mile. There are stretches of swamp inhabited mainly by blacks and malaria mosquitoes, miles and miles of stony desert, pitiless bloodhued ranges, hopeless sandhills, and plains on which the telegraph poles shrink to a needle point and vanish over the curve of the earth. Two years ago bread was two shillings a loaf at Tennant's Creek, and cabbages were three shillings each. Bore water, which sturdily refuses to associate with soap, cost ten shillings a hundred gallons and drinking water was seven-and-six for forty gallons. At Victoria Downs last May the river rose sixty feet and ran through the Australian Inland Mission's nursing home, three feet deep for eighteen hours, leaving behind a deposit of debris eighteen inches deep. One woman in a western district, when I asked how high the river rose, assured me, 'Oh, never higher than two feet in the front bedroom.'

The west is not a woman's country, and the fight a woman puts up to live there is complicated by such things as floods or the dust storms which follow so close on each other's heels that no house stays clean. When the hot weather commences and gastroenteritis enters into its own, drought, dying cattle and a husband somewhere away on a five-hundred mile holding do not make the outback a heaven on earth.

Even in the mid-west, on the plains between Hay and Deniliquin, the wind, particularly in winter, makes the stretch accursed. Half way through the desolation I passed a pitiful little cluster of fallen-down shacks near a weatherboard shanty and asked of the drover leaning on the shanty in the manner of all drovers, 'What do they call this place?'

'This place?' he pondered. 'Oh, it's called Paradise.'

'What on earth made them call it that? Sarcasm?'

He raised his whip and pointed. 'You see them four trees over there? Well, when chaps came driving stock across the plains and saw them trees they reckoned it was Paradise.'

There are women and children living in Paradise. They are living in far worse places, and it would be an easy matter to fill pages with stories of their achievements.

Nevertheless, this does not justify the fond belief cherished by some of our minor statesmen that rough conditions, hard living, poor surroundings result in a virile, energetic race. Not in this climate. There are women, thousands of them, rearing illiterate children in bark huts, drudging in monotonous misery, and they are not rearing a virile race. It is from the more prosperous farms where the food is good that the virile specimens come. That women, particularly in the mid-west, are still in much the same position that their grandmothers occupied is not something to be proud of. It is an economic crime.

When I think of women in primitive conditions I remember a woman who came under consideration, when, in a tiny north-western town, the ladies' committee was arranging the distribution of Christmas cheer.

'That poor Mrs Hassell,' the grey-haired lady in the chair exclaimed. 'You wouldn't believe what a bright, pretty girl she was when he first brought her here. He married her in England and, when the war was over, they came back here. He comes in every fortnight to get his dole, and that's something for him to look forward to, but she hasn't been out of that clearing for at least three years.'

When the truck, laden with fruit, vegetables and provisions, turned up the bumping cart track that wound into the scrub in whose depths the Hassell family had their habitat, it was like plunging back a hundred years in time. The rude, one-room hut built of bark, the pitiful small clearing, the weary, heavy man, unshaven, the wild-eyed, silent children, the woman in a shapeless print gown, inarticulate and abashed at three visitors at once. She had at one time become demented by loneliness and privation, and there had been some talk of 'sending her away', but she was quite harmless, quite broken-spirited.

What a contrast between her and the kindly old lady who had insisted that the truck visit the Hassell holding. She did not plough a clearing in the scrub, not she! Her husband farmed some of the best land in the district and could afford a comfortable bungalow on the outskirts of the town. He was proud of his wife's reputation for 'bein' queer'. Since she had reared her children and had the time and energy she sat on every women's committee the district had. If it was a matter of clearing a dead horse out of the creek, she was ready to prod the shire clerk in to doing it quickly. When there was an agitation for better roads or sewerage for the town or cheaper electric light, a new school house, an extension to the pitiful School of Arts library, she was in the van of the fight. She was president of the Country Women's Association branch, on the hospital board, active in support of immunization against diphtheria. She believed the school should have a radio set, that the unemployed should have free medical attention, and that trees should not be cut down just because they were trees. She was regarded with the respect all savage races extend to harmless lunatics, but few recognized in her a pioneer.

As a field for present-day pioneering the mid-west deserves detailed consideration. The western slopes and highlands are clotted with little towns, often in most inconvenient places, which remain as memorials to the spacious days of the gold-diggings. These either become centres for the surrounding farms or lapse into a crippled senescence, slowly dying off. In 'The Cambaroora Star', Lawson has left us a ferocious picture of 'Cambaroora' when the spirit of the gold-seekers was giving way to the complacency of the storekeepers. 'A better kind of people came to settle in the town . . . And they changed its name to Queensville for their blood was very blue.'

As the western slopes and plains become more and more dominated by the small town, the waste of energy on parochial concerns narrows and intensifies. The farmers' wives tend more and more to conform to the standards of the settlement from which they procure their groceries and ideas. They trudge a mental rut narrower than that their grandmothers trod, with nothing more revolutionary in their lives than a new recipe for lemon cake that the minister's wife served at the church tea. But before joining with Jeremiah, who first concisely summed up life in a western life, let us remember the Country Women's Association.

The CWA is an 'association', an organization of the modern pioneering type, which provides a valuable outlet for the fund of enterprise and energy and hospitality that might otherwise bloom to blush unseen, providing teas for visiting bowls or tennis players. With 18,000 members and 335 branches, 145 younger sets, 112 rest rooms, 50 baby health centres, 39 libraries and several tennis courts and playgrounds, the Country Women's Association has done more to ameliorate the conditions of women in the western districts than almost any other organization. It provides valuable services in the provision of rest homes, emergency and maternity hospitals and maternity wards at district hospitals. Above all it has given the women of the settled parts a generous and worthwhile cause in which to express their aptitude for hard work and their untiring hospitality.

The work of the Country Women's Association in New South Wales is done mainly within a radius of three hundred miles from the capital city, within a region from which comes the greater part of the national wealth, the wool, wheat, fruit and dairy produce upon which our economic life depends. It reveals an astounding lack of national perspective that such regions are so poorly supplied with social services that it is necessary for the Country Women's Association and kindred organizations to raise money for them by entertainments, dances, bazaars and the usual round of charity functions. That this should be taken for granted by the greater part of the community indicates a national attitude as harmful as curvature of the spine.

The corollary to the premise that pioneering still goes on must inevitably be that there are still any number of things in our environment that need improving. This is particularly true of the mid-western towns. In these you may find the grand-daughter and grandsons of the first settlers growing up to find that for them the fields of opportunity have a barbed-wire fence. In too many districts a few big estates ring-bark development. The small farmers cannot scrape together enough from their land to keep all the children, and there is little chance as the boys grow up to take up land for themselves. For many the brightest prospect of regular employment is serving out groceries or drapery in one of the local stores.

Naturally, the young are leaving for the city. Many who point to this 'drift' as one instance of the passing of the 'pioneer spirit' will not realize that a girl or boy who comes to the city, high-hearted at the prospect of becoming a clerk, a school-teacher, a mechanic, is just as brave as the Irish peasant who left his home

in the last century because the family plot could not support all
the family.

The impetus for a new pioneering must come from the people
of the country districts themselves. Cheap, universal elec-
trification, better wage and labour conditions, well-equipped
schools, university and agricultural training colleges, hospitals,
parks, suitable playing grounds, sewerage, libraries, these are only
a few of the things that should come to them as a right, not as
a charity. Pioneer hardships were all very well with difficult
transport and communication. Now that these may be made so
swift and efficient, it is not necessary or desirable for a rural life
to be isolated and full of hardship. Similar geographical conditions
are producing a parallel in our country towns to the small,
narrow, mid-western towns of the USA in the 1890s: a peasantry,
dull and illiterate, numbed by poverty and hard work, and a
trading class, corroded with petty social cliques and dead-end
lives. This need not be. We require only the pioneers who will
clear the mental undergrowth and hack away the dead-wood as
their forefathers did the primitive bush.

Now that I have written this the word 'pioneer' no longer makes
me flinch. It has regained its self-respect. No longer has it hoary,
snow-white whiskers and a gush of self-conscious hypocrisy. It
has a future, it is a young word. I have had to use it so often
in this book that I realize that it is the only word for what it means,
and it means something large and proud and daring. The battlers
keep on battling, and any time that one of them carries through
a brilliant piece of work, a new scheme, today or fifty years hence,
the accolade will still be 'pioneer'.

# DALE SPENDER

## Afterword: In Praise of Kylie Tennant

When in 1987 the decision was made to reprint *The Peaceful Army*, Kylie Tennant was the only one of the contributors still alive. Asked to provide an 'Afterword' to the volume – to sum up the changes over the last fifty years – she readily agreed. Although she was in poor health and keen to complete her latest work of fiction, she nonetheless began 'making notes' on the position of women, literature and the nation in 1988.

Frail though she was, and confined to her hospital bed, she sparkled when she spoke and outlined some of her shrewd and often sardonic observations. She was of the opinion that today's women were once again enjoying some of the status and influence that had been their lot – during the Middle Ages! From her vantage point Kylie Tennant concluded that during the Middle Ages women had been in charge of medical care (a most powerful position) and that their nursing and nurturing values had helped to shape the organization of society. From that time on, an increasingly competitive, commercial and brutal philosophy had emerged, as reflected in medical and social developments. But it was her contention that the pendulum had swung back and that, once again, women's compassionate priorities were making their presence felt in the politics and practices of the nation.

Kylie Tennant's insistence that there has been an improvement is based on personal experience – she defied convention and took to the roads and tramped outback with the unemployed in the 1930s – she learned first hand about the brutality of Australian society earlier this century. It was one reason that she began writing. In her many excellent books (and countless short stories and articles), she has documented the lives of the disadvantaged and the dispossessed, and in her own way she has argued for greater awareness and reform. That there is now a social welfare system – a recognition of the rights of Aborigines, of women, of the poor and underprivileged – seemed to her evidence not only of a better and more just society but also of the increased influence of women's traditional concerns.

This thesis was to be the substance of her 'Afterword' – the achievement of women in Australian society over the last fifty years. Sadly, she was not well enough to complete the task. So what was to have been her testimony to the community contribution of Australian women has become instead a testimony to the achievements of Kylie Tennant and a vote of thanks for her invaluable contribution to the cultural heritage.

When in 1937 the young and promising writer Kylie Tennant wrote the last chapter for *The Peaceful Army*, she was already a woman of decided 'views'. One of them was that 'pioneers' were not just men, or necessarily people from the past. Quite deliberately she set about reclaiming the word 'pioneer' so that she could be comfortable with its connotations: when she suggested that pioneers were those who surveyed their society, saw its deficiencies, and determined to provide the necessities for a better life, she set the scene for her chapter 'Pioneering Still Goes On'. She also provided a definition of her self.

Born in Manly in 1912, Kylie Tennant had eccentric parents (particularly *the* 'parent', her father) and a rather colourful childhood. She also had a disturbing habit of questioning the meaning of life. It was partly her capacity to reject the received wisdom that led to her 'unfinished' education and an assortment of odd-jobs in her youth. At sixteen she started working in the office of the Australian Broadcasting Company (on the top floor of Farmers Department Store), and she later moved into publicity. She wrote advertising copy, worked as a journalist, a bar maid, a kiosk keeper and a typewriter seller, before marrying school-teacher Charles Rodd in 1932.

Her courtship was unusual, her marriage unconventional, and her conduct as a wife virtually unheard of at the time; the new bride was more likely to be found tramping the bush tracks than testing recipes in the kitchen.

Kylie Tennant, who walked through much of New South Wales at various times, vigorously defended this mode of transport for one who wanted to know all about the conditions of society.

Everywhere she travelled, she kept notes; her fiction is based on the facts that she gleaned as she lived with those whom she later represented.

Her first novel, *Tiburon* (1935), was set in a small country town in New South Wales and explored the relationship between the respectable citizens and the social outcasts. A picture of the people whom many decent members of the community prefer to ignore, the novel is much more than a realistic social documentary of the interaction and tensions between the 'haves' and 'have-nots'. The perceptions and passions of the author shine through continually so that although there is an awareness of injustice, and an insight into poverty, pain and despair, there is also an understanding that even in the most distressing circumstances some of the joy of living can find expression.

In writing about deprivation and unemployment during the years of the depression, Kylie Tennant was focusing on an issue that drew the attention of many other women writers. But unlike some of her colleagues, such as Katharine Susannah Prichard and Jean Devanny, she did not write her 'protests' to advocate any one party line. Always distrustful of 'systems' and 'solutions' – seeing 'right' and 'left' as competing sects of the same religion and simple solutions to social ills as so much political cynicism – she was concerned to show some of the chaos of existence and to contemplate some of the individual acts of courage and kindness. This was the philosophy that she wrote and lived; on being thanked for the role she played in providing a Christmas dinner for those who would otherwise have gone without, she responded, 'Just don't be grateful. People owe each other kindness, not just one day of the year. We owe it to each other all the time.'

When *Tiburon* was published, Kylie Tennant was quickly recognized as a new and exciting creative force in the literary world. The novel won the S. H. Prior Memorial Prize and helped to establish the author's reputation for presenting a full cast of Australian characters. But, if she won prizes, there were penalties too; she was portraying her country in a poor light, and there were many who were displeased. 'One person who did not care for the book,' she wrote in her autobiography, *The Missing Heir* (1986), 'was Ken Prior, editor of the *Bulletin*, who told me as I autographed his copy that *Tiburon* was "a bad advertisement for Australia". In those days, perhaps in these days also, writing was considered a branch of publicity – a national publicity if you like. *Tiburon* suggested that something had gone wrong somewhere and that was not the impression a patriot would wish to give in the shining circles of omnipotence in London.'

But Kylie Tennant played her own pioneering part; she would not change her story, and she would not recant or repent. She refused to tell – or sell – only the good news; she assumed the strength and maturity of Australian literature and insisted on presenting her 'facts' no matter how unpleasant. In doing so she made a contribution to the maturity and autonomy of the literature of her native land. But she had to look to England to find a publisher for her work.

It was not perversity on her part to portray the underprivileged, but she certainly sought to register a protest. Kylie Tennant was committed to 'showing things as they really were', and she objected strenuously to what she saw as some of the sentimental representations of bush life that were held to be the essence and the ethos of Australian literature. Nothing but the outpourings of 'Frothblower Murphy', she declared, as she argued for a more responsible and more reflective literature of the country; it was the individual 'not the beer' that she wanted to hear speaking: 'And in Australian writing it is as well to avoid, even in Henry Lawson, the undercurrent of Frothblower Murphy. The sentimentality on one side of the literary coin matches the brutality on the other. This brutality has been made into an ethic: "You got to be able to take it." Whatever happens you take it and if you are bleeding you never let on. You admit to life: "Well, it your round." But you come up for the next, beaten but still in the ring. And you learn to laugh.'

Kylie Tennant wanted a more compassionate society, and she believed that this was linked with the acceptance and appreciation of a more compassionate tone in literature.

Although she didn't ever deny the positive features of rural life, Kylie Tennant refused to idealize the Australian bush. Nor did she make the traditional distinction between the viciousness of the city and the beauty of the outback. Her second, and pioneering, novel, *Foveaux* (1939), was about slum life, and in it Kylie Tennant employed some of the same literary techniques (living in Sydney slums to gather material) and revealed many of the same values that are to be found in *Tiburon*.

*The Battlers*, published in 1941, was a remarkable achievement. A chronicle of the lives of society's 'rejects', who were still unemployed and tramping in outback New South Wales on the outbreak of war, this novel is one of the classics of Australian literature. It too won the S. H. Prior Memorial Prize and the Gold Medal of the Australian Literary Society. Again Kylie Tennant held up a mirror to Australian society and reflected some of the shortcomings of the community and some of the strengths of the human spirit.

Although Kylie Tennant was a serious novelist and recorded some of the personal tragedies of her time, her sense of the comic was never far away. Despite her choice of sombre themes, her novels are by no means depressing; rather through her irreverence, rebellion, and sometimes wicked wit, she affirms the joy of resistance and survival.

*Ride on Stranger* (1943) is the story of the young and isolated Shannon Hicks who, buffeted by the storms of life, looks for a safe place in the world. She searches in many bizarre corners before finding a certain security within herself. With her humour, intelligence, ironic view and quest for the meaning of life, Shannon Hicks is in many respects a portrait of the artist as a young woman. And a wonderful heroine in Australian literature.

That the author of these superb novels is a woman is clear from the perspective that Kylie Tennant adopts. Although she often lived like a man and was often mistaken for a man, some of her specific criticisms of members of Australian society are not ordinarily found in the writings of the male sex. ' . . . I learnt by experience you couldn't be friends with men. They immediately thought you might go to bed with them . . . Any young girl with a trace of compassion finds herself pregnant.'

In the days before jeans, women's slacks (and the pill), Kylie Tennant wore men's pants when out on the track. It was easier. It was also a form of protection. It was her disguise when she travelled with the itinerant bee-keepers to make her notes for her novel *The Honey Flow* (1956).

Kylie Tennant could joke about wearing the pants, she could make light of the advances of men, but behind the mocking remarks was an abiding aim to improve the lives of women, particularly in relation to reproduction. In her fiction and her non-fiction she shows how and why women should have the right to their own bodies, and how and why they need reliable contraception. Sexual exploitation, prostitution and abortion have all been treated in Kylie Tennant's novels, and in such a way that they have opened up debate and the possibility of reform. It is not possible to measure the impact that her fictional characters had upon society, but the death of even one of them from an illegal abortion was a pioneering act of courage on the part of the author and undoubtedly made a contribution to raising social consciousness.

In 1943, her novel *Time Enough Later* was published in New York. A 'romance' that maps the unusual affair between Maurice Wainwright and Bessie Drew, this is a light and lively work; it was followed in 1946 by *Lost Haven*, which is dramatically different in tone. This novel, another documentary about the pettiness of many people in a small country town, raises questions about the possibility of improvement in human terms. But, in 1953, in an abridged version entitled *The Joyful Condemned* and in 1968 in the complete version, *Tell Morning This*, Kylie Tennant re-established herself as the ironic – and troublesome – conscience of the community. During the war when female juveniles who lived with servicemen and conscientious objectors were sent to reformatories and gaol, Kylie Tennant explored some of the reasons and the results of such absurd practices. She got a job in a house of correction and managed to get imprisoned in order to provide authentic details about life 'inside' for this work of fiction. Her exposé of prison, of the narrowness, nastiness and monumental failure of the Department of Moral Rehabilitation, stands as an indictment of officialdom and still has relevance. By presenting a plausible picture of society run by villains while innocents and some of the principled are sent to gaol, Kylie Tennant ensured that such injustice could not go unacknowledged.

The tragi-comic style of Kylie Tennant – her portrayal of so many endearing and enduring characters in such authentic and colourful circumstances – was part of her pattern for promoting a more compassionate community. Although she wanted to entertain her readers – and recognized the necessity of getting and keeping their interest – she was determined that her audience would know things when they finished that they sometimes had not even suspected when they began: 'I built up . . . a technique of using fact as a foundation for broadly comic fiction, which people would read drowsily for entertainment without realizing that my stories were penetrating the subsoil of their minds and presenting a picture of their society.'

That it has been comic fiction that Kylie Tennant has produced could never be in doubt. It is typical of her that, as a joke, she had 'the opinion of the *Communist Weekly* . . . placed as a blurb on the back flap of the jacket of one book, *Ride on Stranger*: "A cynical and slanderous novel. A morbid and contemptuous review of Australian life has never been written . . . it is a scandal that valuable paper should ever have been wasted on this irresponsible nonsense."'

There was one academic, however, who failed to appreciate her sense of humour; he took the blurb seriously and quoted it in 'one pretentious compendium'. To Kylie Tennant such an antic simply confirmed her opinion of academics: although many have disparaged her work, she had a subversive form of revenge. Kylie Tennant confessed that at one time, her husband, Roddy, 'was writing a thesis on the influence of the *Bulletin* on the short story canon in Australia, so I took it over. I must have read nearly all the stories ever published in the *Bulletin*. In the years to come I wrote half a dozen other literary theses for deserving friends who had no literary bent. In those days mathematics teachers and all kinds of teachers who wanted promotion had to write literary theses. Then they learnt them off and were given three hours to reproduce them on paper . . . It seemed an excessively mandarin way of obtaining advancement . . . So I helped. I wrote theses on Thackeray, Chesterton, Conrad and Drinkwater. I also later got into shape Roddy's thesis on the use of pyschoanalysis to education.'

Always ready to expose absurdity and pretension, Kylie Tennant did not, however, always write novels, nor did she confine her focus to the unemployed. Throughout her life she wrote many wonderful plays and tales for young people (see, for example, *The Bushranger's Christmas Eve and Other Plays*, 1959). She also wrote some highly informative and very readable historical volumes including *Evatt: Politics and Justice* (1970) and the remarkable *Australia: Her Story* (1953), which was years before its time (and does not now have the status it deserves).

One of her most characteristic and commendable contributions was her representation of Aboriginal community and culture in *Speak You So Gently* (1959). Here Kylie Tennant qualifies – in her own terms – as a pioneer. She not only insists on putting forward a tough picture of Australian society, which many preferred not to see, but also made available the proceeds from the book to set up scholarship funds for Aborigines.

Kylie Tennant described herself as someone who was 'always on the side of the bull'. In her quest for fair play, she worked for the recognition of Australian writers and the acceptance of an autonomous Australian literature. She supported many aspiring authors, and she toured the country giving lectures on Australian writers and the significance of their work. Contemporary Australians are indebted to her commitment and her art.

She is a great Australian writer. She has taken the stance of 'outsider' and used her art to comment on, and criticize, the rules and relationships of human society. She has given Australians a better view of themselves, a better view of their world, and a better image as self-reflective readers abroad. She has created a cast of characters who could be, and should be, familiar to a wide audience for the insights they provide and the affinities they afford. It is perhaps because pleasure and pain have been such an integral part of her life that Kylie Tennant so persistently links the two in her writing.

In 1938 Kylie Tennant made the point that pioneering work continued. In the following fifty years she put her theory into practice and became one of Australia's best literary pioneers. She took new paths, pushed back frontiers, worked hard to increase the area of consciousness.

And as she built upon the achievements of some of the women who went before – the women who contributed to *The Peaceful Army* and the women whom they wrote about – so can today's women and writers build on the work of Kylie Tennant. She is an essential thread in the tapestry of Australian literature, drawing together the contributions of an older generation with those of the new.

*The Peaceful Army* was published in 1938 as a salutary reminder of women's achievements; it was published in the hope that, once stated, women's record of achievement would be given *permanent* recognition; never again would such a reminder be necessary. But fifty years later there is still the same need to restate the value of women's work: fifty years later there is the same need to make visible the contribution of the pioneering work of Kylie Tennant.

# Notes on Contributors

## Flora Eldershaw    1897–1956

Born in Sydney, she attended Sydney University where she met Marjorie Barnard, who became her literary partner. For twenty years she was a teacher (until the war) and despite the difficulties produced most of her literary work during this period. In 1935 and again in 1943 she was president of the Sydney branch of the Fellowship of Australian Writers. Her address to the English Teachers' Association – 'Australian Women Writers' – was published in 1931 and reveals her support for the validity of Australian literature and for the value of women's contribution within it.

## Marjorie Barnard    1897–1987

Born in Sydney, she was educated at Sydney University, where she met Flora Eldershaw. Marjorie Barnard graduated in 1918 with a first class honours and the first University Medal for History, and, although offered a scholarship to Oxford, she was forced to decline because her father refused permission for her to go. Instead she worked as a librarian at Sydney Technical College until 1935, when she resigned to write full-time. Much of her published work was written in collaboration with Flora Eldershaw (under the name M. Barnard Eldershaw), however, she also published a number of important literary and historical works under her own name. *The Persimmon Tree and Other Stories* was first published in 1943, and reissued in 1985. Her volume, *A History of Australia* appeared in 1962, and *Miles Franklin: A Biography* in 1967. This biography, based on a long friendship remains an important source of information on Miles Franklin. In addition, her critical writings on Australian literature were both substantial and influential in the period from the late

1940s to the early 1960s. She was awarded the AO in 1981; the Patrick White Award in 1983; the NSW Premier's Special Award in 1984; and in 1986 an honorary Doctor of Letters from the University of Sydney. Towards the end of her life she lived in Gosford with her companion Vee Murdoch and their cats.

## 'M. Barnard Eldershaw'

The pen name adopted by Flora Eldershaw and Marjorie Barnard. The beginning of their literary collaboration was marked by the publication in 1929 of their award-winning historical novel *A House is Built*. Four more novels followed – *Green Memory* (1931), *The Glass House* (1936), *Plaque With Laurel* (1937) and *Tomorrow and Tomorrow* (1947), which was later reprinted in unabridged form as *Tomorrow and Tomorrow and Tomorrow* (1983).

Their interest in Australian history was reflected in their non-fiction as well as their fiction: *Phillip of Australia* (1938), *The Life and Times of Captain John Piper* (1939) and *My Australia* (1939). There were other joint ventures – *Essays in Australian Fiction* (1938) – and short stories and radio plays.

Although the speculation about who wrote what persists, details about the circumstances of their literary life are more widely known. Flora Eldershaw lived in at the school where she taught, and Marjorie Barnard lived at home, but together they rented an apartment where they did their writing, entertained their literary friends, and played an active part in promoting Australian writers.

## Mary Gilmore   1864–1962

Born Mary Jean Cameron near Goulburn, she had little formal schooling before becoming a pupil teacher in country towns, including the mining community of Silverton, where she developed her interest in the labour movement. In 1896 she went to Paraguay to participate in a utopian socialist settlement, where she met her husband, William Gilmore. When the socialist experiment failed, the couple returned to Australia and took up an arduous farming existence in Victoria. Mary Gilmore used her writing to contend with some of the difficulties of isolation, and some of her pieces and poems were published before she became editor of the 'Women's Page' of the *Sydney Worker*, a position she held from 1908 to 1931 and which she used to champion the rights of women.

Apart from her prolific (and influential) journalism, her published works include *Marri'd and Other Verse* (1912), *The Passionate Heart* (1916), *The Tilted Cart (1925)*, *The Wild Swan* (1930), *Under Wilgas* (1932), *Fourteen Men* (1934), *Old Days, Old Ways* (1934), *More Reminiscences* (1935) and *Battlefields* (1939). *The Letters of Mary Gilmore* (edited by W. H. Wilde and T. Inglis Moore) was published in 1980. Mary Gilmore deplored the destruction and dispossession of the Aborigines and used her writing to register her strong protest against injustice and inhumanity. For her contribution to Australian life and letters she was made a Dame of the British Empire in 1937.

## Dora Wilcox   1873–1953

A poet and playwright, she was born in New Zealand but moved to New South Wales where she worked as a teacher. Her poems were published in a variety of papers and magazines and in three volumes – *Verses from Maori Land* (1905), *Rata and Mistletoe* (1911) and her book based on her Australian experience, *Seven Poems* (1924). She wrote an ode to celebrate the opening of the federal parliament, for which she won the *Sydney Morning Herald* Prize in 1927. Of the plays she wrote, two were published – *Commander Capston* in 1931 and *The Fourposter* in 1937. She was married to the Australian art historian William Moore.

## Dymphna Cusack   1902–1981

Born in Wyalong, New South Wales, she was educated at Sydney University (where she met her later literary collaborator, Florence James) and then became a teacher with the New South Wales Department of Education. Unfortunately, sickness forced her into an early retirement, but she continued to write – often dictating her work – and became one of the best-selling Australian writers: her books have sold in the millions and have been translated into thirty-four languages.

Her novels have specific social and political themes that are still relevant: *Jungfrau* (1936), a frank and courageous statement of women's sexuality; *Say No to Death* (1951), a compassionate account of terminal illness; *The Sun in Exile* (1955), a bitter attack on racism; *The Half Burnt Tree* (1969), an exposé of some of the motives of the Vietnam war; *A Bough in Hell* (1971), an examination of the dynamics of alcoholism. And many more.

She was a prolific playwright, and many of her works have a political motif; they proved to be extremely popular in socialist countries. *Pacific Paradise*, for example, deals with the issue of nuclear weapons.

She also wrote about people and places abroad – *Holidays Among the Russians* (1964), *Illyria Reborn* (1966) and *Chinese Women Speak* (1958), which has recently been reissued.

Dymphna Cusack collaborated with Miles Franklin to write the highly satirical fictional account of the sesquicentenary celebrations (*Pioneers on Parade*, 1939), and the two wrote a play together about the disgraceful reception of Australian literature in Australia (*Call Up Your Ghosts*, published in the *Penguin Anthology of Australian Women's Writing*, 1988). With Florence James, Dymphna Cusack wrote the superb novel, *Come in Spinner* (1951), a wonderful story about women's existence in Sydney during the second world war.

## Dorothea Mackellar   1855–1968

Best known for her poem, 'My Country', written when she was nineteen, she was born in Sydney and educated at Sydney University before embarking on a life of travel. 'My Country' was published in her first volume of poetry, *The Closed Door* (1911), and this was followed by three more volumes – *The Witch Maid* (1914), *Dream Harbour* (1923), and *Fancy Dress* (1926). She also wrote three novels; *Outlaw's Luck* in 1913 and with Ruth Bedford, *The Little Blue Devil* (1912) and *Two's Company* (1914). She was made a Member of the Order of the British Empire in 1968.

## Eleanor Dark   1901–1965

Born Eleanor O'Reilly in Sydney, she published her first poems in 1921, in *Triad*, as Patricia O'Rane. She lived in Katoomba most of her life, after moving there on her marriage to Eric Payten Dark in 1922. She later disclaimed her first novel, *Slow Dawning* (published in London in 1932), but thereafter received considerable literary acclaim. *Prelude to Christopher* (published in Sydney in 1934) and *Return to Coolami* (1936) each won the Australian Literary Society's Gold Medal. Eleanor Dark was concerned with issues of social justice, and many of her novels are about the meaning of democracy, the motivation for war; *The Little Company* (1945), for example, raises questions about the role of the writer in time of war. Sexual politics and racial politics are the substance of much of her fiction, and *The Timeless Land* (1941), *Storm of Time* (1948) and *No Barrier* (1953) comprise an integrated trilogy on the evolution of Australia with particular reference to Aboriginal culture. *Lantana Lane* (1959) shows Eleanor Dark's capacity for telling a good yarn. A great Australian novelist, Eleanor Dark's work also warrants greater recognition.

## Helen Simpson   1897–1940

Novelist, playwright and historian, she was born Helen de Guerry Simpson in Sydney. She worked as a linguist during the first world war and, on her marriage to Denis Browne in 1927, settled in England but continued to visit Australia until her death. She was a well-established and well-respected writer – producing almost thirty volumes in her forty-three years, some in collaboration with the successful English writer, Clemence Dane – and two of her novels about Australia have achieved international acclaim: *Boomerang* (1932) and *Under Capricorn* (1937), which was filmed in 1949, directed by Alfred Hitchcock and starring Ingrid Bergman.

## Miles Franklin   'Brent of Bin Bin'   1879–1954

Novelist, journalist and fervent feminist, she was born Stella Maria Sarah Miles Franklin near Tumut, New South Wales, and grew up at Brindabella in the Monaro region. That she felt women writers did not receive a fair hearing was one reason for the choice of her pen names. Her best known novel is *My Brilliant Career* (1901), which is a lively and entertaining account of the young Australian woman confronted with the choice of artistic fulfilment or marriage. After its publication she worked as a journalist in

Sydney and was active in literary and feminist circles, where she became the friend of Rose Scott.

From 1905 until the first world war, Miles Franklin lived in Chicago and with fellow Australian Alice Henry became involved in the women's labour movement and with the periodical *Life and Labor*. She worked as a volunteer for a short time during the war and then stayed on in England until 1927, during which time she wrote under the name of 'Brent of Bin Bin', a pseudonym that aroused much speculation in Australia. In 1932 she returned to Australia and in 1936 she won the S. H. Prior Memorial Prize for *All that Swagger*. Partly because she was incensed by the lack of recognition given to Australian writers she wrote (with Dymphna Cusack) the award-winning play entitled *Call Up Your Ghosts*, which satirized the situation. In 1948 she established the Miles Franklin Award for Australian fiction to give visibility and support to Australian literature. She was among the most colourful and committed contributors to the Australian world of letters, and her publications include *Some Everyday Folk and Dawn* (1907), *Up the Country* (1928), *Ten Creeks Run* (1930), *Back to Bool Bool* (1931), *Old Blastus of Bandicoot* (1932), *Bring the Monkey* (1933), *Pioneers On Parade* (with Dymphna Cusack, 1939), *My Career Goes Bung* (1946), *Prelude to Waking* (1950), *Cockatoos* (1954), *Gentlemen at Gyang Gyang* (1956), and *On Dearborn Street* (1981), the last two published posthumously.

## Olive Hopegood   n.d.

No information is available on this writer.

## Winifred Birkett   1897–1966

Born in North Sydney, she published poetry and fiction. *Eidelweiss and Other Poems* was published in 1932. *Three Goats on a Bender* (1934) is an entertaining story about three women trying to breed goats. Other books include *Earth's Quality* (1935) and *Portrait of Lucy* (1938). Her work was highly regarded by her contemporaries, including Mary Gilmore.

# Margaret Preston 1875–1963

Born Margaret Rose McPherson in Adelaide, she moved to Sydney in 1885 and attended Fort Street School and, once determined to study art, began with china painting. She moved to Melbourne in 1892 to further her studies and, in 1894, went back to Adelaide. From 1904 to 1906 she was in Europe, attending for some time the Government Art School for Women in Munich with fellow Australian artist Bessie Davidson. From 1906 to 1912 she was again in Adelaide, supporting herself, in part, by teaching.

In 1912, she returned to Europe (with South Australian painter Gladys Reynell), and she was having some success with her work when war broke out; with Gladys Reynell she taught pottery-making to shell-shocked soldiers. She deplored the destruction of war.

In 1919, she moved to Australia and married William Preston. She played an active part in the promotion of Australian art: she advocated the adoption of an indigenous art that encompassed the native influence (including the Aboriginal) and broke free from the imperial influence; she called for the recognition of the achievement of women artists and found herself in good company; among her friends were the writers Alice Grant Rosman, Mary Grant Bruce and Marjorie Barnard. She challenged the male-dominated bush ethos and produced art that ranged from interior decoration and fabric design to floral arrangement, painting and print-making. In 1932 she contributed to *Ink*, the journal of the Society of Women Writers of New South Wales. In 1933 she opened the exhibition by Alison Rehfisch. In 1934 she contributed to the newly established Women's Industrial Arts Society, and in 1938 she wrote her article on Australian women artists for this volume. She was Australia's foremost woman painter between the wars and exhibited at Royal Academy, New Salon, International Society of Artists, and New English Art Club. She was a foundation member of the Australian Academy of Artists and an exhibitor at the sesquicentenary exhibition.

# Kathleen Monypenny 1894–1971

Born in Hay, NSW she was educated in England, away from her family. As a young woman she returned to Australia and entered the library service, spending most of her working life with the Mitchell Library. In 1931, *Australian Rhyme Sheet* was published in collaboration with other authors, and was followed by five books for children. She was also a reviewer and an occasional broadcaster. During World War II she returned to England to help care for refugee children. A friend of Marjorie Barnard, a posthumous collection of her poems, *Songs of the Lyrebird* was published in 1975, with a short biographical note by Marjorie Barnard. Apart from that, little else is known about her.

## Kylie Tennant   1912–1988

Born in Manly, she worked in a variety of 'odd' jobs before her marriage when she was twenty to the school-teacher Charles Rodd. She continued to gain first-hand experience of 'the seamier side of society' by somewhat unorthodox means: tramping outback with the unemployed, living in Sydney slums, even going to gaol. And she used her experiences to write 'realist' fiction. Determined to document the lives of the disadvantaged who were excluded from the Australian dream, she wrote fiction and non-fiction that prompted concern for reform. Early recognized as a rising literary star (her first novel, *Tiburon*, 1935, won the S. H. Prior Memorial Prize) she still antagonized some critics and academics who disliked the image she presented of Australia.

A prolific writer of novels, plays, articles, reviews, biographies, literary criticism and children's literature, she is quintessentially Australian in her irreverence and plea for a fair deal. She was a highly original writer, but, however, refused to idealize the outback and the bonds between mates. Instead she wrote about the underdogs, women, Aborigines, the unemployed, the old – the dispossessed. And, though she repudiated the social conditions that deprived them of dignity, she did not repudiate the individuals who dealt with difficulties, drudgery, despair. Among her lively and witty novels are *Foveaux* (1939), *The Battlers* (1941), which won the Australian Literary Society Gold Medal and the S. H. Prior Memorial Prize, *Ride on Stranger* (1943), *The Honey Flow* (1956), *Tell Morning This* (1968) and *Tantavallon* (1983). *Speak You So Gently* (1959), an account of Aboriginal communities, *All the Proud Tribesman* (1959), winner of Children's Book Award, and *Ma Jones and the Little White Cannibals* (1967) all show her blend of comedy and compassion.

She was a woman of great sympathy and a writer of considerable skill who was committed to social justice and the women's cause.

## Dale Spender    1943–

Born in Newcastle, she was (poorly) educated in Sydney and taught in New South Wales high schools before taking a position at James Cook University in 1974. In 1975 she moved to London where she lectured at the University of London and took up writing. Her second book, *Man Made Language*, was published in 1980 and is an account of women's silence in a male-dominated society. An undeterred, unapologetic and unhyphenated feminist, she has continued to write about the absence of a fair hearing for women in the construction of knowledge (*Men's Studies Modified*, 1981), in education (*Invisible Women: The Schooling Scandal*, 1982), in the history of ideas (*Women of Ideas – and What Men Have Done to Them*, 1982; *Feminist Theorists*, 1983). More recently she has written about the silencing of women in literature: *Mothers of the Novel* (1986), *Writing a New World: Two Hundred Years of Australian Women Writers* (1988), *The Writing or the Sex?* (1988). In her attempt to redress the balance she has edited series of reprints and compiled *The Anthology of British Women Writers* (with Janet Todd, 1988) and the *Penguin Anthology of Australian Women's Writing* (1988). Concerned to provide women with 'a voice', she has worked to establish publishing outlets, including *Women's Studies International Forum*, Athene Series, Pandora Press and the *Australian Women's Library*. She now spends most of her time in Sydney.

# ACKNOWLEDGEMENTS

The editor and publisher wish to thank the copyright holders for permission to reprint articles in this book: 'Ode To The Pioneer Women' is reproduced from *The Passionate Heart* by Mary Gilmore © Estate of Mary Gilmore 1948 and 1969, with the permission of Angus & Robertson; 'Elizabeth Macarthur–The Happy Pioneer by M. Barnard Eldershaw is reproduced with permission; 'Mary Reiby' by Dymphna Cusack is reproduced with permission; 'Release' by Dorothea Mackellar is reproduced with permission; 'Caroline Chisholm and her Times' is reproduced with permission; 'Rose Scott: Some Aspects of Her Personality and Work' by Miles Franklin is reproduced with permission; 'Pioneering Still Goes On' by Kylie Tennant is reproduced with permission; 'Some Pioneer Women Artists' by Margaret Preston is reproduced with permission; 'A Group of Noble Dames' by Flora Eldershaw is reproduced with permission.

# FOR THE BEST PAPERBACKS, LOOK FOR THE

## PENGUIN

Series Editor: Dale Spender
**The Penguin Australian Women's Library** will make available to readers a wealth of information through the work of women writers of our past. It will include the classic to the freshly re-discovered, individual reprints to new anthologies, as well as up-to-date critical re-appraisals of their work and lives as writers.

### The Penguin Anthology of Australian Women's Writing
edited by Dale Spender

'Only when all the women writers of Australia are brought together is it possible to identify . . . a distinctive female literary tradition.'

Australia has a rich tradition of women writers. In 1790 Elizabeth Macarthur wrote letters home while she travelled to Australia; in 1970 Germaine Greer published *The Female Eunuch*. Thirty-seven writers – working in every genre – are included in this landmark anthology.

Margaret Catchpole
Elizabeth Macarthur
Georgiana McCrae
Louisa Ann Meredith
Catherine Helen Spence
Ellen Clacy
Mary Fortune (Waif Wander)
Ada Cambridge
Louisa Lawson
Jessie Couvreur (Tasma)
Rosa Praed
Catherine Langloh Parker
Barbara Baynton
Mary Gaunt
Mary Gilmour
Henry Handel Richardson
Ethel Turner
G. B. Lancaster
Mollie Skinner

Mary Grant Bruce
Miles Franklin
Dymphna Cusack
Katharine Susannah Prichard
Nettie Palmer
Marjorie Barnard
Eleanor Dark
Dorothy Cottrell
Christina Stead
Sarah Campion
Kylie Tennant
Nancy Cato
Faith Bandler
Nene Gare
Olga Masters
Oriel Gray
Antigone Kefala
Germaine Greer

# FOR THE BEST PAPERBACKS, LOOK FOR THE

## PENGUIN

**Mr Hogarth's Will**  Catherine Helen Spence

Jane and Alice Melville have been disinherited by their uncle, who believes that a 'boys' education will serve them better than an inheritance.

The sisters' struggle for independence and fulfilment takes them from Scotland to Australia and a new vision of their lives.

First published in 1867.

**Kirkham's Find**  by Mary Gaunt

Phoebe Marsden wants a place of her own. At twenty-four she refuses to compromise her ideals and marry for expediency. Her younger sister Nancy does not share her ideals. Against everyone's advice Phoebe decides to set up on her own and keep bees.

Phoebe is one of the first Australian heroines to choose between marriage and a career. Her choice has unexpected ramifications for another sister, Lydia.

First published in 1897.

### Her Selection: Writings by Nineteenth-Century Australian Women
edited by Lynne Spender

Nineteenth-century Australian women writers were published widely in magazines, newspapers and books in Australia and abroad. Their writings provide an insight into the lives of women, the opportunities and obstacles, the hardships and the successes. This lively collection brings together works that have been unavailable for many years.

Included are works by: Georgiana Molloy, Louisa Lawson, Annabella Boswell, Mary Fortune and 'Tasma'.

### A Bright and Fiery Troop: Australian Women Writers of the Nineteenth Century   edited by Debra Adelaide

Who was the most popular detective story writer of the nineteenth century? A woman, Mary Fortune.
Who was the internationally famous botanist and artist who also wrote novels? A woman, Louisa Atkinson.
Who wrote the first convict novel? A woman, Caroline Leakey.
Who wrote the first novel with an Aboriginal protagonist? A woman, Catherine Martin.

This book opens up the hidden history of Australian literature and is the first critical appraisal of the major Australian women writers of the nineteenth century.

The book includes photographs.

# FOR THE BEST PAPERBACKS, LOOK FOR THE

## PENGUIN

**No place for a Nervous Lady**
*Voices from the Australian Bush*   Lucy Frost

A fascinating collection of previously unpublished, intimate letters and diary entries by thirteen women in nineteenth-century Australia. It captures the fearful isolation of life in the bush and the marvellous friendships that developed between correspondents.
A McPhee Gribble/Penguin Book

**The Penguin Book of Australian Autobiography**   John and Dorothy Colmer

A lively and stimulating introduction to more than forty Australians who write of their own lives. They include Kylie Tennant, Patrick White, Joan Lindsay, David Malouf, Miles Franklin, Henry Lawson, Judah Waten, Henry Handel Richardson, Charles Perkins, Stella Bowen, Donald Horne, Oriel Gray, Albert Facey, Clive James, Robin Eakin, George Johnston and Mary Gilmore.

## BOOKS BY THEA ASTLEY IN PENGUIN

### Hunting the Wild Pineapple

Leverson, the narrator, at the centre of these stories, calls himself a 'people freak'. Seduced by north Queensland's sultry beauty and unique strangeness, he is as fascinated by the invading hordes of misfits from the south as by the old-established Queenslanders.

Leverson's ironical yet compassionate view makes every story, every incident, a pointed example of human weakness – or strength.

### It's Raining in Mango

Sometimes history repeats itself.

One family traced from the 1860s to the 1980s: from Cornelius to Connie to Reever, who was last seen heading north.

Cornelius Laffey, an Irish born journalist, wrests his family from the easy living of nineteenth-century Sydney and takes them to Cooktown in northern Queensland where thousands of diggers are searching for gold in the mud. The family confront the horror of Aboriginal dispossession – Cornelius is sacked for reporting the slaughter. His daughter, Nadine, joins the singing whore on the barge and goes upstream, only to be washed out to sea.

The cycles of generations turn, one over the other. Only some things change. That world and this world both have their Catholic priests, their bigots, their radicals. Full of powerful and independent characters, this is an unforgettable tale of the other side of Australia's heritage.

# FOR THE BEST PAPERBACKS, LOOK FOR THE

## PENGUIN

### Rooms of Their Own

Interviews by Jennifer Ellison with:

Blanche d'Alpuget
Thea Astley
Sara Dowse
Helen Garner
Elizabeth Jolley
Olga Masters

Jessica Anderson
Jean Bedford
Beverley Farmer
Kate Grenville
Gabrielle Lord
Georgia Savage

*Rooms of their Own* is a collection of interviews with twelve authors of contemporary Australian fiction.

Jennifer Ellison's rapport with the writers and their writing has elicited surprisingly frank views on the relationship between authors and publishers; the place of writers in society; the role of gender in writing; and many other issues. Together, the interviews form a dynamic account of the creative, professional and personal motivations of some of Australia's most important living writers.

### The Penguin Book of Australian Women Poets

Edited by Susan Hampton and Kate Llewellyn

This anthology represents eighty-nine Australian women poets, from tribal Aboriginal singers through to the present.

The range of subjects and styles is as wide as the differences in the lives of the poets. There are poems about the selector's wife and daughter, factory work, prostitutes, social conventions, feminism, lovers, Japan, old age, happy marriage, the conflict between love and independence, and the Sydney Harbour Bridge. There are poems that do not exist in official histories, as well as poems that have come to be regarded as classics.

*The Penguin Book of Australian Women Poets* presents for the first time an overview of the traditions, the voices and the range of women's poetry in Australia.